ESSENTIALS OF

STAGE LIGHTING

ESSENTIALS
OF
STAGE LIGHTING

HUNTON D. SELLMAN
California State University, San Diego

APPLETON-CENTURY-CROFTS
Educational Division
MEREDITH CORPORATION
New York

CONTENTS

v

ILLUSTRATIONS

PREFACE

In this first separated version of the stage lighting part of *Stage Scenery and Lighting*, the author has continued his intention to write a handbook for a technical director and lighting designer as well as a beginning textbook for a college class in stage lighting. Several new chapters have been added. There has been some demand for a brief chapter on the history of lighting in the theatre, and a short one on this subject has been included. Rather than merely dropping in bits of information about basic fundamentals of illumination where they seem to fit best, this material has been introduced as a separate chapter, keeping it to the most elementary and bare essentials.

Each aspect of the material has been brought up to date and enlarged in places while keeping all of the material as simple and elementary as possible. Since the use of projections has been greatly expanded in the production of plays in recent years, it was thought worthy of a separate chapter. To broaden the point of view in the final chapter on the practice of lighting plays, the writer has included two examples from the Broadway theatre as exemplified by the work of Professor Donald Oenslager and the late Jean Rosenthal. An enlarged glossary of stage lighting terms and the usual bibliography and list of manufacturers will be found at the end.

The writer wishes to acknowledge the assistance of Dr. and Mrs. Gordon Howard and Professor Walter Stump for helpful comments on Chapter 2, Dr. Merrill Lessley, Professor Donald Oenslager, and Miss Eleanor Denny for material in Chapter 9, Priscilla M. Sellman in helping with many rough places throughout the manuscript, and Mrs. Frances Hill for typing and comments.

He wishes further to thank the following people and organizations for many of the illustrations: Century Strand; Henry Klopot, Kliegl Bros.; Joel Rubin and Bruce Kelly, Electro Controls; General Electric Large Lamp Dept.; Charles Clark, the Major Corp.; Superior Electric Co.; Skirpan Lighting Control Corp.; Sylvania Electric Products; Strand Electric; Phillip Rose; Ward Leonard Electric Co.; Professor John Conway, University of Washington; Professor

Arnold Gillette, University of Iowa; Professor Kenneth Graham, University of Minnesota; Professor Horace Robinson, University of Oregon; Professor Don W. Powell, California State University, San Diego; Professor Gary Gaiser, Indiana University; and Professor Peter Marroney, University of Arizona.

H.D.S.

ESSENTIALS OF

STAGE LIGHTING

Figure 1–1 A scene from Eugene O'Neill's, *Emperor Jones*. University of Arizona, 1966. Direction by Peter Marroney. Design and lighting by Robert Burroughs. (Photo Courtesy Department of Drama, University of Arizona.)

AN INTRODUCTION TO STAGE LIGHTING

CHAPTER 1

INTRODUCTION

Theatre is a collaboration of many arts, in which a group of artists attempts to communicate with a group of people—the audience. Through sight and hearing, the director, the actors, the scenic and costume designers, and finally the lighting director try to tell a story or share an experience with an audience. George Pierce Baker said that the drama is the shortest distance between emotion and emotion. The actor, through his interpretation of the play, brings the thought and emotion of the drama to the intelligence and emotion of the audience.

The other artists necessary to the production support the actor

1

and aid him in bringing a consistent interpretation of the play to the audience through sound and light. Adolphe Appia said, "Living art implies a collaboration."[1] Light reveals the scenery, the actor, and his costume and blends them into a living, moving aesthetic expression. Light guides the eye, focusing attention; or by its absence it deliberately conceals the extraneous. Light sets the actor apart from his background and communicates the time, the place, the season, and the mood. It not only discloses the whole composition, it sometimes becomes the composition itself.

BACKGROUND

Adolphe Appia, distinguished revolutionary in design and light at the turn of the last century, pointed the way in his writings and stimulating designs.[2] He called the familiar light of his time (from borderlights and footlights) general illumination (*Helligkeit*). According to Appia this kind of light was useful, perhaps, but inadequate; there must be a new kind of light, a form-revealing light (*gestaltendes Licht*) to give objects on the stage their natural three-dimensional quality—there must be living light for living people.[3] From Appia's *gestaltendes Licht* the contemporary concept of specific illumination has developed.

Recent developments in incandescent lamps and the improvements in design and construction of instruments and their control have not made Appia's ideas obsolete. Even today artificial light can be divided into two kinds, which correspond to the two kinds of light in nature. Direct sunlight is a shadow-producing, form-

[1] Adolphe Appia, *The Work of Living Art and Man is the Measure of All Things,* translated by H. D. Albright (Coral Gables, Fla.: University of Miami Press, 1960).

[2] Adolphe Appia, *Die Musik und die Inscenierung* (Munich: F. Bruckman, 1899).

[3] Many years ago (1925), when I read Appia's *Die Musik und die Inscenierung,* I came across the word *"gestaltendes,"* which according to German dictionaries means "formative." Since light does not actually form an object but reveals its form, I adopted the term "form-revealing light" as the best way of getting at Appia's meaning. In 1962 an authoritative translation appeared: Adolphe Appia, *Music and the Art of the Theatre,* translated by Robert Corrigan and Mary Duglas Dirks (Coral Gables, Fla.: University of Miami Press). In this book the two terms are translated as "diffused light" and "living light." Since the translators had access to the German publication and also the original French manuscript, I assume that "living light" is nearer to Appia's intention. He probably intended a more emotional connotation, since he referred to "diffused light" as producing mere visibility and to "living light" as being more expressive.

revealing light that may be called *specific* illumination. In the theatre, or on the stage, specific illumination is produced by spotlights. The other kind of light, general illumination, like sky light in nature, is a shadowless illumination produced on the stage satisfactorily by striplights and floodlights. Through the influence of photography and television, two synonyms for general and specific lighting have come into use: key light for specific illumination and fill light for general illumination. When these two kinds of light are properly produced, controlled, and distributed according to good stage lighting standards, the basis for effective results has been established.

CONTROLLABLE PROPERTIES OF LIGHT

These two kinds of light have three properties—quantity, color, and distribution—over which varying degrees of control are possible. The quantity of light is controlled by the number of sources of light, their size, dimming control, and color filters. From the point of view of the audience, the quantity or amount of light influences visual acuity, fatigue, and mood. The amount of light needed for the stage has always been determined by a mixture of guesswork and experience. More research is needed, but good judgment has helped to establish a reasonable range of illumination for the stage. Acting area illumination ranges from 1 to 150 lumens per square foot.[4] These figures mean very little, of course, unless such factors as color, reflectance, contrast, size of an object, distance from the observer, and the nature of the surface are known. For short periods of a few minutes, 1 lumen per square foot on fairly light objects might be satisfactory in a moonlight scene. At the other extreme, 150 lumens per square foot in a bright scene in a musical comedy would not be unusual. For plays a somewhat lower level of illumination would be expected; perhaps 5 to 25 lumens per square foot for a serious play and 25 to 50 in a bright comedy would be common.

Such obvious things as avoiding glare by preventing very high contrast and removing bright sources from the sight of the audience should always be remembered. A sufficient amount of light to prevent eye fatigue should of course be provided on an acting area. When members of the audience are straining to see with insufficient light, they frequently miss important parts of the play. Since mus-

[4] A lumen per square foot, or a foot-candle, is the illumination on a surface 1 foot from a source of 1 candle power. The usual illumination meter indicates illumination in foot-candles, which is numerically equal to lumens per square foot (see Chapter 3).

cular control of the iris in the eye and changes in the retina, called adaptation, require time, we must control changes in illumination accordingly, especially in going from light to dark. For example, an audience can see a dimly lighted scene more clearly (and with less strain) if the house lights are dimmed slowly and if the house is left dark for a few seconds before the curtain rises than if the house lights are snapped off and the curtain is opened immediately. The reason for this is that adaptation takes place in a few seconds when light becomes brighter, but it takes as much as several minutes for adaptation from light to dark. Everyone has had the experience of stumbling about for a while upon entering a cinema theatre from bright daylight. A number of quick changes of scene with widely different levels of illumination will tire an audience much more rapidly than lighting slowly changed, or kept at a single level of illumination, because in the first case the eye has been over-worked. There is evidence that higher levels of illumination make people more alert, and we know by experience in the theatre that audiences enjoy a sophisticated comedy in bright light more than they do one in which the lighting is at a lower level. Bright light for comedy and dim for tragedy is an old but useful rule.

The control of *color* is just as important as the control of quantity of light. In producing plays in the sixteenth century, not only was quantity of light different in comedy and tragedy, but colors differed also. Warm colors were used for comedy and cool ones for tragedy. This conception of color is still in general use today, but there are many exceptions in which color is used intelligently in defiance of this rule.

In working with color on the stage, one is interested in it both objectively and subjectively. Objectively, a *source of light* is selected, modified, and reflected before it reaches the eyes of the audience. On the other hand, the director is more interested in how color affects the minds of individuals in the audience. This is the subjective, or psychological, aspect. The color of the source is modified by the reflector, lens, and color filter, and by some means of dimming. This controlled color is further modified by the reflecting surfaces of scenery, properties, make-up, and costumes before it reaches the eye of the observer, who sees the final result as a pattern of color. Mixing colors additively by dimming and varying the proportion of colors from two or more sources is another phase of color control. The discussion of color continues in Chapter 6.

Distribution is the term used to indicate the way in which light of any quantity or color is spread (distributed) over the acting area and the background. Obviously, the three controllable properties are closely interrelated. Distribution depends upon the use of both kinds of light, specific and general, to produce different levels of illumination on the acting area and on the scenery, and upon variety in color over the same surfaces. The fact that scenery, costumes, properties, and even the actors' make-up vary considerably in their ability to reflect light, and in the way they reflect it, is a highly important consideration in the lighting distribution for a play. Even when an actor moves about the stage he changes the distribution of light, because his body and costumes are reflectors like any part of the setting. A successful distribution of light on the stage depends on the length and angle of the shadows, the depth of shaded areas and their contrast with highlights, and the difference in levels of illumination, without the extremes which are sometimes called "dead spots" and "hot spots." These last are merely evidences of too much contrast, or insufficient blending of general illumination with specific illumination and insufficient overlapping of lighted areas.

Thus the controllable properties of light take their place in an analysis of stage lighting. In a single sentence the whole matter can be expressed like this: Both general and specific illumination can be controlled and changed in quantity, color, and distribution to accomplish the five functions of stage lighting discussed in the following section.

THE FUNCTIONS OF STAGE LIGHTING

The functions of stage lighting are generally agreed upon by those who work in the theatre, but the names of the functions and their divisions differ somewhat. For purposes of discussion the functions are divided here into five:

1. Selective visibility
2. Revelation of form
3. Illusion of nature
4. Composition
5. Mood

1. Selective Visibility

The most important thing that light can do on the stage is to allow an audience to see comfortably and clearly. Visibility depends upon the amount of illumination, the size of the lighted objects, the amount of light an object reflects, contrast with its background, and the distance between the object and the observer. This is a general statement, applicable to the stage as well as elsewhere. Obviously, light should at all times be sufficiently bright for comfortable vision without fatigue; but large numbers of people work and read every day under insufficient illumination. The theatre is only a minor offender in this respect, but settings are frequently seen in which extreme contrasts are annoying. For example, table and floor lamps are frequently too bright and sky cycloramas are very often too light in contrast to the level of acting area lighting. On the other hand, many productions are lighted with insufficient contrast; in other words, everything on the stage is evenly and monotonously illuminated. The mean between these extremes is preferred, and visibility is a matter of degree. That is, visibility must be selective if the audience is to see what it is intended to see at any moment.

In a recent production of Giraudoux's *Ondine*, the first-act cottage was placed about 30 inches above the floor to suggest that it was on the edge of a mysterious lake in an enchanted forest. The cottage was isolated in space by means of selective lighting until the "sister" ondines appeared from under the cottage and in two narrow beams of light near the downstage corners of the cottage. As they tried to seduce Hans, the cottage nearly disappeared, because Hans and the three ondines were lighted by separate narrow beams of light (see Chapter 9).

By lowering the level of illumination, visibility can be reduced until an object completely disappears or is left inconspicuously in shade or shadow until one wishes to have it reappear. This method of lighting is always effective with a permanent set when changes are made by moving from one part of the stage to another. Color too is concerned with visibility. Under ordinary lighting conditions visibility reaches the maximum in yellow and drops off in blue, green, orange, and red. Because of this fact, higher levels of blue light are necessary for a night scene than would be needed if yellow light were used. On the other hand, monotonous, uniform distributions of blue light in large quantities quickly bring fatigue to the eyes of the audience.

Quoting Appia again, "If there is no shade there is no light . . . light is distinguished from visibility by virtue of its power to be expressive. If there is no expression, there is no light."[5]

2. Revelation of Form

Revelation of form, easily ignored and overlooked, is what Appia called "living light," the light that must be expressive. When plays

[5] Appia, *Music and the Art of the Theatre*, p. 75.

are lighted with general illumination alone, actors, properties, and pieces of scenery all look flat and uninteresting. There are no high-lights, no shadows, no variety in the distribution of light. The walls of a set have as much light on them as the actors' faces have, and in fact every object, every surface, is at the same level of illumination. This is anything but form-revealing light. In order for objects to appear in their natural form, the distribution of light must have a high degree of variety produced by different levels of illumination. In the first place, there must be that form-revealing, shadow-producing light which we call specific illumination. Appia said that shade and shadow are equal in importance to light itself. In one of the notebooks of Leonardo da Vinci there appear some pertinent comments on the subject. He says, "Shadow is the withholding of light. It seems to me that shadows are of supreme importance in perspective, seeing that without them opaque objects and solid bodies will be indistinct both as to what lies within their boundaries and also as to their boundaries themselves. Consequently I treat of shadow and say in this connection that every opaque body is surrounded and has its surface clothed with shadows and light." And again, "Excess of light makes things seem hard; and too much darkness does not admit of our seeing them. The mean is excellent." One of the fundamental demands of depth perception is the harmonious relationship between the scenery and the actor, and the way light contributes to this relationship. For example, if the angle of illumination and the position of the actor are such that the shadow of the actor falls halfway up Mount Whitney on the drop, any sense of depth is immediately destroyed, and any sense of theatrical illusion is reduced to a ludicrous absurdity. The scene designer can paint a natural haziness in the outlines of the distant objects, and light can participate by keeping distant objects dimmer than those in the foreground. As discussed under the subject of projected scenery, the slides for projection (both for lens and Lin-nebach projectors) can be made to suggest objects at different dis-tances by the sharpness or softness of their outlines.

Separation of the actor from his background, even from the wall of a set 10 feet behind him, is a highly important part of the func-tion of form revelation. It can be done in three ways. First, the background should have considerably less light, perhaps one-fourth to one-twentieth of the light on the actor. Furthermore, the light on the background should be general illumination. The actor, as men-tioned above, should be lighted with specific illumination. The second factor in depth perception is the use of some intense, specific illumination from the side, avoiding high levels of general illumination or monotonous levels of specific illumination from the front. The third method, so common and so effective in television, is back lighting, with specific illumination highlighting the hair of the actress as well as her shoulders and neck. If back lighting is impossible, some sources directly overhead will aid in separation and in the perception of depth.

Revelation of form, then, is accomplished essentially by specific illumination. But specific illumination monotonously applied can easily approach general illumination in making a scene flat, dull, and uninteresting. The angles and direction of specific illumination, together with carefully applied highlights balanced by shade and shadow, make the difference. Contrast and variety in color also are a part of this difference that compels the interest and attention of the spectator.

3. Illusion of Nature

Illusion of nature includes the use of artificial light to create the illusion of natural light that indicates time of day, locale, and season. It includes also the simulation of artificial illumination in interiors to indicate light from chandeliers, bracket lights, and other luminaires commonly found in interiors. These are merely *motivations* (apparent sources) for the actual acting area lighting and are almost never used as real sources of light for the acting area. The sources of outdoor and interior illumination are also a part of design.

By the amount of light and the color, one can distinguish between the intense tropical sunlight of a South Sea island and the weak cold sunlight of northern Norway. With the same variables the romantic moonlight in *Cyrano de Bergerac* can be differentiated from the cold moonlight in *Mourning Becomes Electra*. In plays of naturalism, and perhaps sometimes in plays of realism, the vertical angle of sunlight and moonlight may be important. In a play with a single set, suppose that the first act takes place in the morning with the sunlight coming in a window at stage left. In the second act the time is mid-afternoon, and the angle of the sun will be different and will enter through a different window. A sunset should not be seen through the same window where the morning sun appeared. The length of shadows may be important in certain plays to indicate the time of day, and foliage patterns on the walls of buildings assist in this function as well as in that of composition.

The color of sunlight is actually almost white, or at least it is a very much lighter tint of yellow than unmodified incandescent light. While cool white sunlight might help create an appropriate mood for tragedy and melodrama, it would not have sufficient contrast for comedy. In keeping with the theory that theatrical exaggeration increases the effectiveness of all the elements of dramatic production, the amber color for sunlight has become an appropriate convention for comedy. Varying from a pale greenish yellow (usually unpleasant for comedy) to a pinkish or orange yellow, a shaft of sunlight is considered a pleasing motivation for the acting area light. It should be placed and directed not only for this function but also for design, in so far as its pattern falls on the walls of a set or other objects.

Moonlight, too, is concerned with color. Natural moonlight, as everyone knows, is sunlight reflected from the surface of the moon, and accordingly is yellow in hue. But if one used yellow moonlight on the stage, it would be confused with sunlight and would also be a distraction because of its "unconventional" color. It is reasonable to suppose that the cool color for moonlight developed as a convention because of its association with the blue night sky. Shafts or beams of moonlight produced with spotlights are conventionally some tint of blue, depending on the taste or discretion of the artists concerned. They might be anything from greenish blue to lavender blue, the latter being good for very romantic scenes. "Steel" blue or pale blue-green are the usual colors for moonlight.

4. Composition

Composition is the use of light as an element of design. If one turns a borderlight and footlights on three walls and a few pieces of furniture, he illuminates a box set and the first function, visibility, may be accomplished. But if one can succeed in creating, according to the principles of good design, a distribution of light, with variations in quantity and color, he is composing a picture with light. This requires general illumination of the right tonality and quantity; it requires specific illumination from an angle best suited to each object, so that the highlights are accurately placed and the shadows are massed and formed as a part of the design. Shadow patterns, too, are useful for design as well as for representations of nature. Design in light is not static like a painting in oil or water color, but is a mobile painting in space, changing continually and following the drama as an accompaniment. Lighting should focus the attention of the audience and build a new design with every movement of the actor.

Light, as an element in stage design, may vary from a projected image on a cyclorama with only actors in front of it, to a design in space with no reflecting background at all. The director builds the composition with actors, and light reveals his composition as a mobile design. With a small amount of dust or reflecting vapor in the air, the design may be extended to include the shafts and cones of light from spotlights. In a simpler way projected images on a cyclorama or drop may become a part of a design with other elements of wood and canvas. Light, motivated by sunlight or moonlight, may be a pattern of foliage or grill work decorating a wall. Light may isolate a small group of actors into a unit, by ignoring the rest of the set and moving with them from place to place, thus forming a whole series of compositions as the scene develops. Without light, design cannot exist; and without design, lighting is only illumination.

5. Mood

Mood includes the emotional and psychological impressions that light can add to the spectators' appreciation of a play. Being somewhat intangible, this may be difficult to achieve. The lighting designer must, of course, be well aware of the mood and the changing moods of the play, coordinating his activities with those of the other artists concerned. In addition to his theatrical opportunity for study, a student pursuing this subject would do well to examine the works of painters such as Leonardo da Vinci, Rembrandt, Munch, and van Gogh, concentrating on the means by which they heightened their concepts through the modulation and direction of light.

The first four functions of light discussed are interdependent, and each is related cumulatively to the overall mood. For example, sharp contrasts in specific illumination employed for selective visibility create highlights and dark shadows, which will sharpen the impact of a mystery or melodrama. An intense amber sunlight augments the feeling of oppressive heat above and beyond merely providing an indication of the time of day. While light by itself can create an effective composition, at the same time it should provide simultaneously for the spectators' aesthetic enjoyment. To move them emotionally, an oversized or distorted shadow can be made to incite fear and the shadow of a cross may enhance religious feeling. Even the common concepts of bright, warm illumination for comedy and dim, cool light for serious drama are obviously relevant to this function. Such efforts to enhance the mood of a play with light should be well integrated. Unity and clarity are highly important in any theatrical production, since each contributing idea must be firmly established as part of the overall design.

Figure 1–2   A scene from *Sergeant Musgrave's Dance*. University Theatre, University of Oregon. Direction by Herbert Kline. Design by James Ellingwood. Lighting by J. Thibeau.

The contribution of light to the creation of mood should be a subtle thing that affects the audience without calling attention to itself. The red sunset in Euripides' *Hippolytus* may coincide with the messenger's report of the death of Hippolytus, but if it attracts more attention than the messenger's speech, the sunset is a distraction rather than a reinforcement of the mood.

CONCLUSION

The way in which the kinds of light, the controllable properties, and the five functions are applied to the specific examples of Giraudoux's *Ondine* and Genet's *The Maids* will be found in Chapter 9. Along with the various principles involved in using light for the stage, the instruments and equipment needed to produce and control illumination will be found in the intervening chapters.

THE HISTORY
OF STAGE LIGHTING

CHAPTER 2

INTRODUCTION

For 2000 years our theatre needed no other light than the sun. During the Italian Renaissance, however, the theatre gradually began to move indoors. The spectacles, pageants, and plays frequently produced in the palace gardens were more and more being done inside the great halls of the ruling nobles, and leading artists of the day, such as Michelangelo and Leonardo da Vinci, were called upon to design and supervise these spectacles. The first permanent "classic" theatre, the Teatro Olimpico (which survives to this day in Vicenza, Italy) was designed by a famous Italian architect, Andrea Palladio. Built between 1580 and 1584, the stage

12

and auditorium were originally open to the sky, and no stage lighting as we know it was planned. The first theatre with a proscenium
and curtains, the Teatro Farnese, was built at Parma about 1618.

Leone de Somi, in his *The Means of Theatrical Representation*
(about 1550) presented an idea still practiced in theatres today:
He provided "full illumination of those scenes in a tragedy in which
the subject matter was happy, but when the first unhappy situation
occurred, he found means to shade or extinguish many of the
sources of light. In the auditorium he placed very few lamps, and
these were behind the spectators so that light would not interfere
with their view of the stage. Little is known about the illumination
of these performances other than that the sources of light were the
torches, cressets, candles, and crude oil lamps commonly employed
for the activities of everyday life.

In 1545, when an architect and painter named Sebastiano Serlio
brought out Book II of his *Architecttura,* he described the scenery
of his time and explained how the stage and scenery were lighted.
In a specific application of these illuminants to the theatre, he suggested that colored light could be produced by putting colored
liquids in bottles—such as red wine, obviously, for a red light,
ammonium chloride in a copper vessel for a blue light, and saffron
for a yellow light. By using a brightly polished barber's basin behind
a torch or candle, he developed an elementary spotlight with a round
bottle serving as the lens. Color changes could be made with little
effort by changing the liquid.

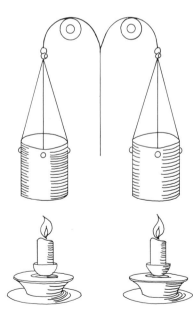

Figure 2–1 A sixteenth century dimming device composed
of metal cylinders that could be
lowered over candles. (From
Sabbatini, *Practica de fabrica
Scene e Machine ne'Teatri,*
1638.)

In 1638, Sabbatini's *Practica de fabrica Scene e Machine ne'Teatri* provided an ingenious dimming device which lowered metal cylinders over candles (Figure 2–1). Another Italian architect of the time, da Vignola, suggested that the ideal angle to light an object was along the diagonal of a cube.

In Germany in 1628, an architect called Joseph Fürtenbach described a stage sloping toward the audience. In front was an orchestra pit with a wall masking the musicians from the audience. On the stage side of this wall was a row of oil lamps that later were called footlights. On each side of the stage were wings with a vertical row of oil lamps attached to the stage side. About this time Fürtenbach is said to have made a trip to Italy, and it is possible that he saw footlights positioned in this manner in an Italian theatre.

In England toward the end of the sixteenth century and the early part of the seventeenth, the Elizabethan public playhouse[1] was the principal place for theatrical production. It was, as we all know, an outdoor theatre but there were a number of indoor ones, too, the best known being the Blackfriars. In these theatres candles were the principal source of light. Around 1600 elaborate masques were very popular at court; the two best-known names associated with them were Ben Jonson and Inigo Jones. Jones, born in 1573, made two extended trips to Italy and returned to become the best-known designer of these extravaganzas. He brought back many ideas from Italian theatres, including the proscenium arch and improved uses of light, probably including footlights.[2] They became known as "floats" or floatlights some years later because one type consisted of containers of oil with floating wicks. Overhead were suspended rings or hoops with rows of candles around the circumference. Jones increased his "brilliant" effects by the use of gold and silver

[1] In outdoor theatres such as the Elizabethan public playhouses, artificial lighting was used in the form of candles and torches to suggest time and place according to the demands of the play. Candles were carried in and out of rooms or placed on tables to suggest that the time of a scene was after dark. Many Elizabethan plays had scenes that needed this indication that the actual time of the scene was at night because the whole play was presented in the afternoon.

[2] W. J. Lawrence doubted the frontispiece for *The Wits, or Sport upon Sport* as issued in 1663 and said further in his *The Elizabethan Playhouse and Other Studies* (reissued in 1963 by Russell and Russell, Inc., New York), "But we have no evidence of the regular employment of footlights in the English theatre until the third or fourth decade of the eighteenth century." While I may be presumptuous to disagree with such an authority, it seems reasonable to me that footlights came to England from Italy and France along with many other theatrical details in the seventeenth century.

in the decorations. His productions were highly elaborate, and the expenditure of large sums of money on them seems to have been no problem.

In Paris during the seventeenth century, at the Hôtel de Bourgoyne, six crystal chandeliers were suspended over the stage and a row of little lamps formed the footlights. Molière, at the Palais-Royal, had 12 chandeliers, each with 10 candles hanging over the stage, and 48 candles in his footlights. When the English theatre was restored in 1660, it was influenced strongly by ideas from France. Unfortunately, nearly all of our information about the lighting of the English restoration theatre is from lists of material and labor, and it is impossible to determine which was for the auditorium and which was for the stage. For example, for a theatre called the Cockpit in Court a list includes "twenty fair gillt branches with three socketts in each for candles." For a masque in Whitehall in 1675, 96 tin sconces and tin plates for reflectors were required. Sconces and candlesticks were even nailed to the backs of "clouds."

In the well-known frontispiece to The Wits[3] published in 1672, one can see two-branched chandeliers and a row of six small oil lamps with double burners, clearly a row of footlights. An engraving of the Red Bull in about 1673 shows footlights at the edge of the stage. In a list of preparations for a masque in 1670 or 1671 is an item "making a trough at the foot of the stage for lights to stand in." Later, the trough became a long narrow sheet-metal box with a masking reflector on the audience's side. In this box a number of cotton wicks running through large round pieces of cork floated in oil, "floats" or "floatlights."

This stage extended almost entirely in front of the proscenium arch and most of the light for the actor came from the chandeliers overhead, supplemented by the floatlights or a row of candles at the edge of the stage. These obviously illuminated the audience as well as the actor. Candles behind the proscenium were used to light the scenery. Many of the actors' exits and entrances were from proscenium doors on each side of the forestage, with some theatres having as many as six of them. In France in the second half of the seventeenth century, Torelli and Vigarani introduced many elaborate scenic and lighting effects from Italy. One French theatre, the Salle de Machines, apparently could stage anything a designer could imagine and included the latest in lighting and pyrotechnic displays.

In the eighteenth century in England, the great actor-manager,

---

[3] The Wits, or Sport upon Sport, was a collection of short comedies acted in private halls during the Puritan ban of the theatres between 1642 and 1660.

David Garrick, is credited with many improvements and changes in stage lighting. In fact he is said to have brought back many ideas from France, where lighting and technical innovations were considerably ahead of those in the English theatre.

Garrick, who became manager of the Drury Lane Theatre in 1747, dominated the British stage until his retirement in 1776. He probably deemphasized the apron or forestage by moving some of its lighting behind the proscenium arch, adding winglights and borderlights, and arranging the lighting on the main stage so that actors were willing to stay behind the curtain line. Garrick brought a French scene designer, Howard de Loutherbourg, to Drury Lane, whose new ideas for scenery and light proved to be exceptional for their time.

Candles dominated the lighting of the eighteenth century until the kerosene lamp with an adjustable cylindrical wick was invented in France in 1783. A glass chimney for this lamp soon increased its usefulness and helped to allay the constant fear of fire.

In New York, the historic John Street Theatre, erected in 1767, was typical in that it followed European examples. It was lighted by candles for 30 years, during which attendants were required to trim the wicks, and many complaints were made of candle snuffers performing their functions during inopportune moments of dramatic tension.

These difficulties were soon to disappear, for William Murdock, an English engineer, developed in 1791 a method of making illuminating gas in quantity. In 1803 Frederick Albert Windsor used gas to light the Lyceum Theatre in London, and gas came to the American stage in 1816 when a system was installed in the Chestnut Street Theatre in Philadelphia. At first there were no municipal gas plants and theatre managers had to manufacture their required amount, which is one reason gas did not come into general use for theatrical productions until the middle of the nineteenth century.

Gas lighting was indeed a great improvement in stage lighting, not only in increased brightness but even more in the control it permitted. Miles of rubber tubing from outlets in the floor called "water joints" carried the gas to borderlights and winglights (Figure 2–2). But before it was distributed, the gas came through a central distribution point called a "gas table." Here the degree of brightness could be controlled, and dimming could at last be accomplished. On the other hand, there were some disadvantages: Several hundred theatres are said to have burned down in America and Europe between 1800 and the introduction of electricity. The increased heat was objectionable, and the borderlights and winglights had to be

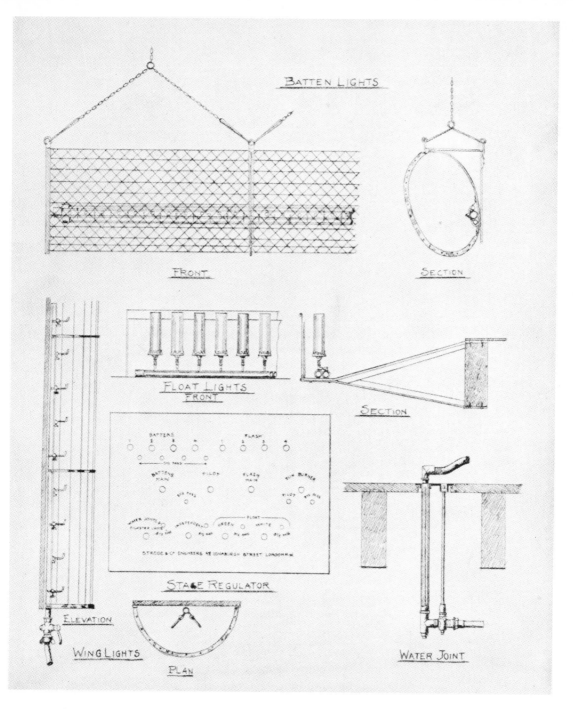

Figure 2–2 Details of gas lighting equipment taken from *Building News,* Oct. 1894. This illustration shows construction of batten lights, winglights, and footlights, and indicates layout of the control board from which the dimming and brightening of the lights were manipulated. [From *Theatre Lighting—Past and Present* (Mount Vernon, N.Y.: Ward Leonard Electric Company, 1928).]

Figure 2–3 A block of lime heated to incandescence by an oxy-hydrogen blow pipe was used for many years as a spotlight in the theatre. From this practice the expression "to be in the lime light" originated. [From *Theatre Lighting—Past and Present* (Mount Vernon, N.Y.: Ward Leonard Electric Company, 1928).]

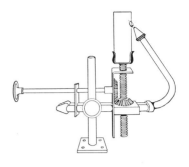

lighted by a long stick with a flaming wad of cotton at the end. For many years an attendant or gas boy moved along the long row of jets lighting them individually while gas was escaping from the whole row. Both actors and audiences complained of the escaping gas, and explosions sometimes resulted from its accumulation. By 1860 the jets were lighted with an electric spark and glass chimneys were added, especially to the footlights. In 1890 a gas mantle was invented, with a thorium oxide-impregnated gauze "mantle" being placed in the gas flame. This improved the quality as well as the amount of light produced by illuminating gas.

About 45 years earlier Henry Drummond had discovered that by heating a piece of lime to a high temperature with a flame produced by oxygen and hydrogen it became incandescent and emanated an intense white light. While this lime light required constant attention by an operator, it lent itself to use as a spotlight by the addition of a lens and metal housing. Its adjustment is shown in Figure 2–3. This intense source concentrated by a lens made it useful for sunlight through a window, moonlight, or as a "follow spot." Several of these were used to light the stage from the auditorium, much as "balcony front" lighting is done today. Lime light was in common use by 1860.

In an article in *The Nineteenth Century* magazine,[4] Bram Stoker reviewed Sir Henry Irving's contribution to lighting. Irving managed the Lyceum Theatre in London from 1878 to 1898, during which he had two mains for gas brought into the theatre in case one might fail. Up to this time, the auditorium usually remained "brightly" lighted during a performance, but Irving is said to have started the practice of dimming the house lights before the curtain opened.[5]

[4] Bram Stoker, "Irving and Stage Lighting," *The Nineteenth Century*, Vol. 69, May, 1911.

[5] This had been done for special effects before this time.

Very little had been done to change the color of gas light before Irving became manager. "Mediums," "woven films of cotton, wool or silk drawn between the lights and the stage" were available, but they were dyed in only a few colors. Irving and his employees began to have transparent lacquers applied to the lime lights, and when electricity came in he had it applied to the bulbs of the incandescent lamps. In the footlights he used separate rows of different colored lamps, with some rows divided into sections. In this way he could throw any part of the stage into greater prominence, which amounted to a crude type of "area lighting." Irving seems to have begun the practice of lighting rehearsals scheduled late at night, for he spent long hours working out the lighting of each scene with his large staff of technicians when actors were not present.

Arc lights, like lime lights, required personal attention, but Paul Jablochkoff by 1878 introduced an arc in the form of an electric candle that required no attention at all. It was made of two carbon sticks side by side with an insulating material between (Figure 2–4) that burned away at the same rate as the carbons. In 1879 a theatre in France was equipped with some of these, but they appeared too late to come into general use.

Electricity had already come to the theatre by way of the Paris Opera in 1846. As shown in Figure 2–5, an electric arc was located at the focal point of a parabolic reflector to represent the rising sun in a production of *The Prophet*. In 1860 at the Paris Opera, an electric arc spotlight such as is shown in Figure 2–6 was used in a production of *Moses*.

During the nineteenth century a number of inventors were working on an incandescent electric lamp, but it was not until 1841 that the British government granted the first patent on an incandescent lamp to Frederick De Moleyns. J. W. Starr patented the Starr-King

Figure 2–4   The first really commercial arc lamp was the so-called Jablochkoff candle, which consisted of two carbon electrodes insulated from each other by material that was broken down and consumed by the arc as the electrodes wore away from the action of the arc. [From *Theatre Lighting—Past and Present* (Mount Vernon, N.Y.: Ward Leonard Electric Company, 1928).]

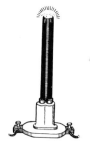

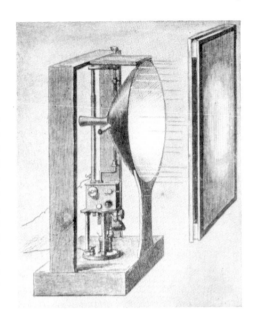

Figure 2-5 Apparatus used to represent an artificial sun in the production of *The Prophet* in the Paris Opera in 1846. An electric arc was located at the focus of a parabolic mirror and the beam of parallel rays projected on a silk screen. This was the earliest authentic application of electric light on the stage. [From *Theatre Lighting—Past and Present* (Mount Vernon, N.Y.: Ward Leonard Electric Company, 1928).]

lamp, which contained a stick of carbon. Sir Joseph W. Swan made a number of experimental lamps between 1848 and 1860 and later became one of the foremost manufacturers of incandescent lamps in England. Thomas Edison is usually credited with inventing the incandescent lamp in America in 1879, but other inventors also made contributions. The filament in Edison's first lamp was a carbonized bamboo fiber, and for a few years the incandescent lamp remained

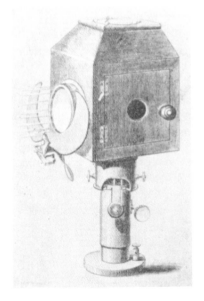

Figure 2-6 The first electric spotlight was apparently the one shown here. It was employed in the Paris Opera in connection with the production of *Moses* in 1860. [From *Theatre Lighting—Past and Present* (Mount Vernon, N.Y.: Ward Leonard Electric Company, 1928).]

Figure 2–7   Cross section of electrically lighted theatre constructed in Munich for the International Electro-Technical Exposition in 1882. This was a remarkable installation which inspired theatrical managers all over the world. Arc lamps were used in the auditorium—the lamps themselves being invisible and their light transmitted through a skylight—a system of lighting which is still popular. The electrician who operated the dimmer may be see at the side, his dimmer being located on the floor below. Footlights, battens, winglights, and bunchlights are all shown in action. [From *Theatre Lighting—Past and Present* (Mount Vernon, N.Y.: Ward Leonard Electric Company, 1928).]

a low-power, dull-red carbon filament inside a glass bulb from which most of the air had been withdrawn.

As shown in Figures 2–7 and 2–8, a theatre lighted by electricity was constructed for an exposition in Munich, Germany, in 1882. This stimulated much interest among theatrical managers, and electric lighting almost immediately replaced gas at the Savoy Theatre in London and at the Bijou Theatre in Boston.

Many theatres rushed to change from gas to electricity, but there were several problems. One was heat for the audience as well as for the stage. Gas had provided this heat, but after the changeover,

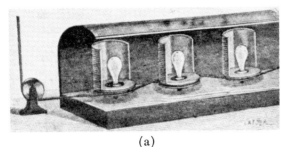

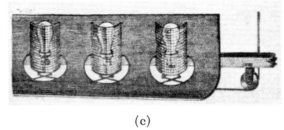

(c)

(a)

(b)

Figure 2–8   (a) Detail of footlights shown in Figure 2–7. These lamps were connected with a dimmer for regulation of intensity. Change in color was also provided by mechanical means, each lamp being fitted with a revolving screen, one section of which gave the natural light, the two other sections being blue and red, respectively. The change from one color to the next was made by pulling a cord so connected as to turn the screens.

(b) Detail of winglights shown in Figure 2–7. The color of the light from these lamps was changed by hoisting and lowering color screens. Like all the other lamps in the theatre, these were also connected to a dimmer.

(c) Detail of batten light shown in Figure 2–7. These lamps were controlled in the same way as those described in part (a). [From *Theatre Lighting—Past and Present* (Mount Vernon, N.Y.: Ward Leonard Electric Company, 1928).]

audiences complained of "freezing" and another means of heating for physical comfort had to be provided. Another problem was comparable to that of the early days of gas—no central generators. By the end of the century every city had its own central gas works, but now the theatres that had changed to electricity had to have individual electrical generating plants installed.

A third and very important problem was concerned with the control of the amount of light for the performance. It had been easy with gas, but difficulties arose with the new source of energy. One of the early solutions, the so-called "salt-water" dimmer, required a large container of water, such as a barrel with a handful of common salt. One insulated wire with a metal plate at the end was placed at the bottom of the wood, glass, or ceramic container, and the other wire with a metal weight attached was lowered until the two metallic contacts touched, bringing the light full up. Increasing the distance in the water between the metallic ends of the wire increased the resistance to the flow of current through the lamps, and accordingly the lamps became dim. This worked considerably better for outdoor productions, because chlorine gas was given off at one electrode and containers of water can be a bit messy on the stage.

Figure 2–9 Dimmer rheostat and control board shown in the foreground of Figure 2–7. Note that this dimmer provided individual control for each rheostat by means of a lever handle. These handles could also be attached to a longitudinal bar operated by a slow-motion wheel from the front. In this way independent control or interlocked control was obtained. [From *Theatre Lighting—Past and Present* (Mount Vernon, N.Y.: Ward Leonard Electric Company, 1928).]

In a few years an electrical dimmer called a *rheostat* was devised (Figure 2–9). Figures 2–10 and 2–11 show early models. This rheostat consisted of a length of high-resistance wire (German silver or, later, nichrome) arranged in a coil with a sliding contact to introduce more or less of the wire in series with the lamps. Rheostats were large and clumsy at first. In Germany the large-resistance dimmers (rheostats) were placed in the basement and controlled by flexible steel cables brought through holes in the stage floor.

As early as 1890 it was demonstrated that dimming could be done by reactance. Figure 2–12 shows a system in a theatre in London in 1896. In this illustration an iron core attached to a leather strap was lifted in and out of a coil of copper wire. When the core was out of the coil, the lamps were bright; by lowering the core into the coil the lamps were dimmed.

These two methods of dimming incandescent lamps, resistance and reactance, were the two common methods for many years. When direct current was the source of power, resistance was the only method of electric dimming. While resistance has been obsolete for many years where alternating current is available, road companies continue to carry portable resistance control boards for reasons of economy (a few years ago an autotransformer portable board was carried with a road company of *My Fair Lady*). Many resistance systems are still in use because they are still in good operating condition. They work with either direct current or alternating current, whereas reactance dimmers and all other methods operate on alternating current only. Refinements of the reactance system continued through the 1940's. In fact, a relative of reactance, the magnetic

Figure 2-10 Early Ward Leonard Vitrohm Theatre Dimmer made up of two Vitrohm rectangular plate units, connected together and mounted on a panel board which carried a dial switch with an extension lever to permit convenient adjustment. These dimmers were installed in Altmeyer's Theatre, McKeesport, Pa., in 1892. [From *Theatre Lighting—Past and Present* (Mount Vernon, N.Y.: Ward Leonard Electric Company, 1928).]

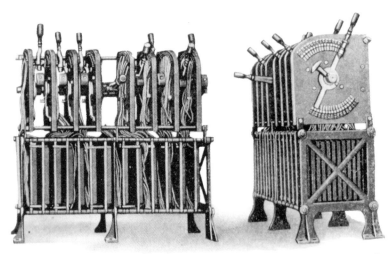

Figure 2-11 Ward Leonard Theatre Dimmer put on the market in 1894. It consisted of banks of Vitrohm rectangular plates mounted in a framework above which dial switches were arranged. Connections between the contact points on the dial switch and corresponding points in the resistor units were made by means of wires. This was the first step in decreasing the space occupied by a bank of theatre dimmers. [From *Theatre Lighting—Past and Present* (Mount Vernon, N.Y.: Ward Leonard Electric Company, 1928).]

Figure 2–12
An early form of reactance dimmer used in Earl's Court Exhibition Theatre and described in *London Engineer,* Nov. 1896. In this installation special attention was paid to the switching from one color to another. As one color decreased in brilliancy, the succeeding color was simultaneously increased in brilliancy. The arrangement shown here permits individual setting of different circuits and also gives interlock and operation with a slow-motion worm and wheel, or by means of a master lever. Detail of master lever and slow-motion worm and wheel is shown in upper right-hand corner. [From *Theatre Lighting—Past and Present* (Mount Vernon, N.Y.: Ward Leonard Electric Company, 1928).]

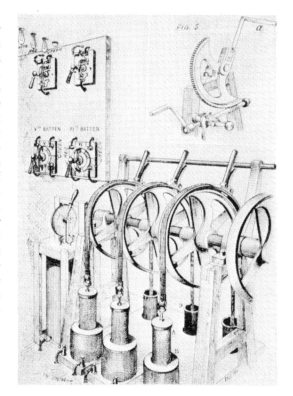

amplifier, continued to be specified by engineers and architects (in competition with other systems of dimming) until the 1960's.

Very few improvements in resistance dimmers were made between the clumsy model of 1897 (Figure 2–13) and 1910, when Ward Leonard made circular dimmers with 110 dimming steps. Figure 2–14 shows the distribution of wire before the protective enamel coating was added. Each was about 17 inches in diameter, with 3000 watts capacity. About this time dimmers were set on edge in rows above the switchboard, and connecting rods were brought down to handles in a row just above the top of the switchboard. The handles were attached to a steel shaft in a way that allowed the dimmers to be operated individually or by a longer heavy handle as a group. This was called *mechanical interlocking.* In this way the whole stage or a part of it could be dimmed with one or two hands.

Before 1920 the switchboard itself consisted of an insulated panel with open knife switches on the front. This was called a "live-front" board because one could come in contact with the copper current-carrying electric parts. This, for obvious reasons, is illegal today.

In the 1920's the "dead-front" board became common. The switches were placed behind a rigid nonconducting panel, with

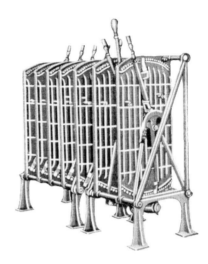

Figure 2–13 Bank of Ward Leonard plate dimmers (1897) arranged for individual control as well as master control. The master lever is between the first and second plates. [From *Theatre Lighting—Past and Present* (Mount Vernon, N.Y.: Ward Leonard Electric Company, 1928).]

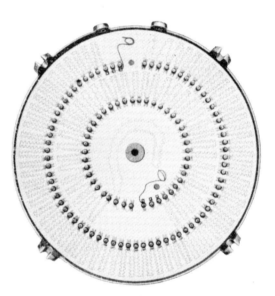

Figure 2–14 Vitrohm Dimmer Plate before the application of protective enamel coating to resistance wire and contact button. Note particularly the wide area covered by the resistance wire on the metal plate. This aids materially in securing rapid dissipation of heat developed during use from the entire metal base. [From *Theatre Lighting— Past and Present* (Mount Vernon, N.Y.: Ward Leonard Electric Company, 1928).]

their insulated operating handles protruding through slots to the front of the panel. About the same time the dimmers were placed in rows directly behind the board, so that the dimmer and switch for each circuit were close together. Pilot lights were added to indicate at a glance that a circuit was "on."

In the mid-1920's two more improvements appeared. For large circuits or for a master switch (one controlling several or all of the circuits) another switch opened and closed by an electromagnet was placed in the basement and a small switch to operate the electromagnetic one took its place beside the dimmer. Soon each circuit had a set of tiny switches (5 to 10—sometimes even 20) that could be switched on in advance to set up each circuit in preparation for a specific scene. The manufacturers told the customer that now one could produce a play with 10 or even 20 scenes and change the lighting from scene to scene by the flick of one master switch. What they "forgot" to mention was that the operator had to go over the whole board between scenes and reset all the dimmer readings. These switchboards, sometimes 20 feet long, were anything but simple to operate, but they were soon to be superseded.

In the mid-1930's the autotransformer dimmer succeeded the resistance dimmer (for alternating current) for direct-control systems. Refer to Chapter 8 for more information about autotransformers. They are not obsolete even today for direct-control systems under circumstances in which economy is of the greatest importance. Unfortunately, the larger sizes occupy as much or more space than the obsolete resistance dimmers, although electrically the autotransformer is far more satisfactory. For rugged service and strict economy it is still a choice worth considering for a small control board.

About this time or a few years earlier, the reactance dimmer came back into prominence through the application of electronics. While the reactance dimmer had been used occasionally on high-wattage circuits (but requiring too many resistance plates), a separate 110-volt direct-current supply was needed to control it. In the early 1930's a control circuit with a thyratron tube was developed which made it desirable to use this type of dimmer on all of the circuits in a remote-control system. Only small potentiometers were needed to operate the dimmer manually. With refinement this became the most desirable dimmer for remote control until the late 1940's. This dimmer came to be known as an *electronic reactance dimmer.*

Several years after World War II, Mr. George Izenour developed the use of large electronic tubes as dimmers and the Century Lighting Corp. (now Century Strand) manufactured his system. The Strand Electric Co. of London and Kliegl Bros. in New York produced a slightly different electronic dimming system. The magnetic amplifier succeeded the electronic dimmers. And last, the silicon-controlled rectifier (SCR) or thyristor is the only remote dimmer specified in new lighting systems. In fact, all of those mentioned in this paragraph as well as the electronic reactance dimmer are remote controls placed in a room where space is not a problem, and the manual part of the operation is from a console usually at the rear of the auditorium but sometimes left or right on stage near the proscenium arch.

CONSOLES

Returning to 1930, the late Professor Stanley McCandless designed an organ console-type control board for Severance Hall in Cleveland, Ohio. Built by Westinghouse, it had preset dimmers, master and submaster dimmers, and even foot-pedal controls which could be used when the operator's hands were full. All controls were within the reach of one man and the console had the further advantage of portability; it could be plugged in backstage or moved to one of the auditorium aisles for rehearsals.

This started a trend toward compact consoles for remote systems where the actual dimming and switching was done in a remote area such as a room in the basement. General Electric built such a system with the console under the front edge of the stage in an opera house in Chicago two or three years later. The operator was able to see the stage through an opening in the footlights. Other compact consoles were placed in or near the orchestra pit and a few were placed at the rear of the auditorium, which has proved to be the best place of all.

Parts for the console have been reduced in size so that now individual switches and dimmers are no more than an inch wide. Master controls are a bit larger. In the last 10 or 15 years consoles have not changed very much, even though the remote dimmer has changed considerably. Punch cards have been tried and, recently, preset or multiscene arrangements have been made with platens or thin metallic cards representing a group of dimmers. Two cards can be set in place in advance while others are being reset. The latest development in lighting consoles is a small compact unit related to a computer in which 500 to 700 readings or cues can be stored and instantly recalled at the operator's manual command. Various mastering and fading devices are, of course, included (see Chapter 8).

LIGHTING AND INSTRUMENTS

Very few real improvements in lighting instruments, except the change from gas to electricity, took place between 1875 and 1930. There were the usual borderlights, footlights, and bunchlights, or floodlights (called *olivettes*) manufactured throughout the years with minor changes to suit lamp improvements, and arc spotlights were more important than incandescent ones until 500- and 1000-watt lamps with concentrated filaments came along between 1915 and 1920. Complaints against footlights were heard as early as the mid-nineteenth century, but they were strongly favored by many directors for 70 years more. Gradually their use diminished, until nowadays they are rarely employed, except in revivals of period plays.

Except for the addition of a reflector, the conventional spotlight changed very little until the late 1930's, when the Fresnel lens replaced the plano-convex lens in the majority of instruments. The Fresnel takes its name from a Frenchman who invented a cylindrical lens to surround the source of light in lighthouses in the nineteenth century. Its recent application appeared in ordinary spotlights as a flat round lens consisting of concentric rings with a small plano-convex lens at the center. Each ring is an outer part of a plano-convex lens of short focal length; all of the rings have about the same focal length, which can be shorter than comparable plano-convex lenses. With the shorter focal length the spotlight housing can be shorter, and since the Fresnel lens is cast and not ground, it costs less. Without increasing the thickness, some of them have diameters as large as 12 to 14 inches.

In the mid-1930's a radical new spotlight employing an ellipsoidal reflector that included a much larger solid angle of light came on the market. Spotlight efficiency increased from 8 or 10 percent to 25 or 30 percent (see Chapter 4 for more details). Over the years a few improvements have been made and larger sizes have appeared, but the instrument has remained essentially the same. It is now our most important instrument.

A few years ago the conventional spotlight was redesigned to use a modified ellipsoidal reflector instead of a spherical one. Manufacturers claim that the efficiency has increased from 10 percent to 60 percent at flood focus.

When borderlights were changed from gas to electricity, little improvement took place beyond the substitution of a lamp socket for a gas burner. In the 1920's individual reflectors were added for each lamp. One of the early models was called "X-ray," and glass color media were available instead of lacquer on the lamp itself. Soon a combination spherical-parabolic reflector came into common use for borderlights and footlights that had a colored glass "roundel" to close the opening at the front of the reflector. During the 1930's the practice of cutting borderlights into short sections 6 feet in length became common. This was particularly helpful for lighting the cyclorama from the bottom, because the short sections could parallel the cyclorama about 6 feet from it. Many of these 6-foot sections, now called *striplights*, are made without reflectors because they use a reflector lamp. They are available in several sizes (see

Chapter 4). Borderlights have almost disappeared from use in the modern theatre.

The "bunchlights" of the turn of the century were so called because only small-wattage lamps were available and these floodlights contained about 10 sockets. As incandescent lamps grew in size, box lights called *olivettes* replaced bunchlights (see Figure 2-15) as floodlights on telescopic stands. Later (1930's), floodlights were made more directional and more efficient with parabolic or ellipsoidal reflectors.

The manufacturers of lighting instruments have probably influenced the incandescent lamp manufacturers from time to time. There were many demands for larger wattages for spotlights, and the new ellipsoidal one required a lamp that burned base up. By far the most significant development in incandescent lamps in 50 years, the tungsten halogen lamp, is now about 10 years old. It is still undergoing many changes and improvements. By introducing iodine or another halogen vapor into the bulb, blackening was almost eliminated and the efficiency of the lamps greatly increased

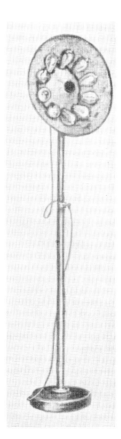

Figure 2-15 Bunchlight made up of incandescent lamps in special bowl reflector as used in 1898. [From *Theatre Lighting—Past and Present* (Mount Vernon, N.Y.: Ward Leonard Electric Company, 1928).]

(see Chapter 4). The stage lighting companies have quickly taken over the new lamp, and many design changes have appeared in lighting instruments.

The engineers who made the development of instruments possible were owners and associates of such pioneering lighting and control manufacturers as Century Lighting (now Century Strand), General Electric, Kliegl Bros., Major Corp., Strand Electric, and Ward Leonard Electric. A number of other firms have recently moved into the field.

Among the men who belonged primarily to the theatre itself, Sir Henry Irving's achievements have already been mentioned. In America during the nineteenth century, Steele Mackaye, the playwright, actor, and inventor of lighting and mechanical equipment, must be mentioned. He had patents on shadowgraph projectors (before Linnebach), theatre seats, and rising, sinking, and floating stages. In Europe in the twentieth century, Gordon Craig, Adolphe Appia, Fortuny, Basil Dean, Max Hasait, and Adolphe Linnebach contributed to the field of stage lighting, while in this country David Belasco, the producer, and his chief electrician, Louis Hartman, gave more attention to lighting the stage than anyone else up to 1920. They stimulated the development of larger and better lamps for spotlights, and they built many instruments and effects in their own laboratories. A man who was devoted to detail, Belasco built bridges over the proscenium arch and employed individual operators for many instruments. He also rehearsed the lighting of his plays for 2 or 3 weeks.

Another devoted individual, a Boston architect named Munroe R. Pevear, developed the use of blue, green, and red, the "primary colors," for the cyclorama and the acting area. He also improved the optics of spotlights, floodlights, and cyclorama footlights. Pevear went into the manufacture of these instruments for the theatre, notably a "tormentor hood," a soft-edge spotlight that was common in many theatres for years, including the Theatre Guild in New York.

Many scene designers of the 1920's such as Claude Bragdon, Lee Simonson, Norman Bel Geddes, and Robert Edmund Jones took a particular interest in light as an integral part of design. There are many others, but two more must be mentioned. The late Thomas Wilfred, inventor of the Clavilux, did more than any other man to develop a separate creative art of light. One of his moving color projectors is still operating at the Museum of Modern Art in New York City. Mr. Wilfred worked in the theatre from time to time and developed a direct beam projector and a lens projector that are very efficient. And this chapter would not be complete without giving due credit to the late Stanley R. McCandless, whose ideas and imagination have contributed more than any other to the careers of those who work in theatre and television lighting in America. He spent most of his professional life as Professor of Stage Lighting at Yale University and a number of years as a designer for Century Lighting. Through his books and his students, his influence on stage lighting is everywhere.

This has been but a brief survey of the history of stage lighting. Of course, it has merely scratched the surface, but a longer account would be out of proportion in a beginner's textbook on the subject as it is practiced today. It is hoped that this backward glance will stimulate the reader to examine the present with a look toward the future.

Progress has been painfully slow at times, although there were two great leaps forward—from oil and candles to gas, and then from gas to electricity. Instrument design and improvement have depended on improvements in the electric incandescent lamp, and control has depended on developments in electronics. Television and educational theatre have helped broaded the market and move the industry forward at a significant pace. Science and engineering are helping make technical progress in an art where there is always much that can be done.

FUNDAMENTALS OF LIGHT AND ILLUMINATION

CHAPTER 3

INTRODUCTION

For a better understanding of stage lighting instruments, their light sources, and their general usefulness in the art of lighting, it is helpful to understand a few fundamentals of light, its nature, and its measurement. Some definitions of terms in the physics of light and in simple illuminating engineering will also add to the clarity of the whole matter.

In illuminating engineering, light is defined as *visually evaluated radiant energy*. Light sources such as the sun and our common illuminants, including the candle, arc light, and incandescent lamp, seem to radiate visible energy in waves. They are designated in what is called a *visible spectrum* in wavelengths measured in angstrom units, the violet end beginning at 4000 angstroms and extending through blue, green, yellow, orange, and red to about 7600 angstroms. Of course, there are invisible wavelengths shorter than blue called ultraviolet, and invisible wavelengths longer than red, called infrared. We are familiar with some of the shorter wavelength energy from the sun that produces "sunburn" on our skins. The infrared energy we frequently call heat.

MEASURING LIGHT AND ILLUMINATION

Any discussion of measurement in illumination starts with a source. In this case one starts with a very small source called a *point source,* with a candle power or luminous intensity of 1 candela (formerly called candle) placed at the center of a hollow sphere with a radius of 1 foot. It is assumed that this source will emanate light equally in all directions. The area on the surface of a sphere is $4\pi \times r^2$ and if r is 1 foot, the area is 12.57 square feet. The luminous intensity of 1 candela will produce 1 lumen (the unit of luminous flux) on 1 square foot of the inside surface of the sphere. Then the source of 1 candela produces 12.57 lumens on the whole surface. Since it has 1 lumen per square foot at any point on this surface, the illumination on the surface is said to be 1 foot-candle as long as we are measuring distances in feet. The common illumination meter measures or indicates the illumination on a surface in foot-candles, which are numerically the same as lumens per square foot. The foot-lambert is the unit of luminous reflectance from a surface. If the illumination on a surface is 10 foot-candles and the reflectance of the surface is 50 percent, the luminance or reflected light from the surface is 5 foot-lamberts.

INVERSE SQUARE LAW

If the sphere mentioned above is 2 feet in radius instead of 1 foot, its surface area is $4\pi \times 2^2$ (12.57 $\times$ 4) or 50.28 square feet, four times as large. If the radius is 3 feet, then the surface is nine times as large, and so forth. With the same source of 1 candela, the density or illumination is decreasing as the square of the distance. This is called the *inverse square law.*

Candle power (cp) = foot-candles (fc) $\times$ distance squared (D^2)

$$48 \text{ candelas} = \text{fc} \times (1 \text{ foot})^2$$

$$\frac{48}{1} = \text{fc} = 48 \text{ foot-candles}$$

$$48 \text{ candelas} = \text{fc} \times (2 \text{ feet})^2$$

$$\frac{48}{4} = 12 \text{ foot-candles}$$

$$48 \text{ candelas} = \text{fc} \times (4 \text{ feet})^2$$

$$\frac{48}{16} = 3 \text{ foot-candles}$$

So it should be clear that the illumination drops off according to the square of the distance.

CONTROLLING LIGHT (OTHER THAN DIMMING)

In stage lighting practice (other than by dimming), light is controlled by reflection, absorption, transmission, and refraction. When light falls on a white opaque surface, most of the light is reflected and a little is absorbed. An opaque surface is one that light does not pass through. If the opaque surface is black, most of the light is absorbed and very little is reflected.

When a beam of light falls on a flat polished metallic mirror, the angle of reflection is equal to the angle of incidence. This is also called *specular reflection* and is shown in the first rectangle in Figure 3–1. Curved reflectors of various shapes are much more common in controlling light in stage lighting instruments. A spherical mirror is shown in Figure 3–2 and parabolic ones in Figure 3–3. The ellipsoidal reflector is shown in Figures 3–4 and 3–5. These are all regular, or specular surfaces.

Diffuse reflection shows no highlight or bright spot but looks equal in brightness from all angles. Scene paint is a good example of a diffuse reflecting surface; Figure 3–6(a) shows how light behaves on a diffuse material. Figure 3–6(b) shows a spread reflecting surface. The reflected beam leaves the surface at the angle of incidence but is spread in a wider pattern than the incident ray. The mixed pattern of Figure 3–6(c) shows a definite highlight leaving the surface at the angle of incidence while most of the light is diffused in all directions. While surfaces with this highlight are usually avoided on the stage, borrowed furniture frequently shows some mixed reflection. Anything owned by the theatre that is used as furniture and properties is ordinarily diffused with steel wool or similar material.

The light that falls on a surface but is not reflected is absorbed. No surface reflects 100 percent of the light that falls on it. Neither is there an opaque material that is so black that all of the light is completely absorbed. Spotlights, for example, would be improved

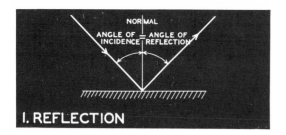

1. REFLECTION

NORMAL

ANGLE OF = ANGLE OF
INCIDENCE   REFLECTION

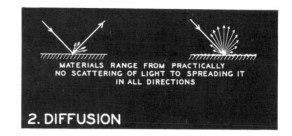

2. DIFFUSION

MATERIALS RANGE FROM PRACTICALLY
NO SCATTERING OF LIGHT TO SPREADING IT
IN ALL DIRECTIONS

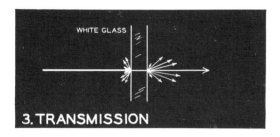

3. TRANSMISSION

WHITE GLASS

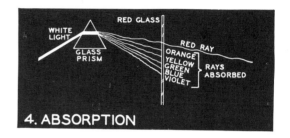

4. ABSORPTION

WHITE
LIGHT

GLASS
PRISM

RED GLASS

RED RAY
ORANGE
YELLOW
GREEN
BLUE
VIOLET

RAYS
ABSORBED

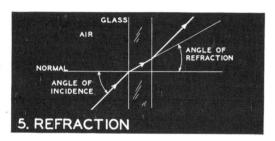

5. REFRACTION

GLASS

AIR

NORMAL

ANGLE OF
INCIDENCE

ANGLE OF
REFRACTION

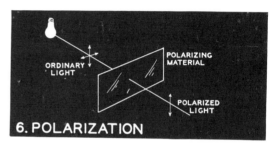

6. POLARIZATION

ORDINARY
LIGHT

POLARIZING
MATERIAL

POLARIZED
LIGHT

Figure 3–1   The usual means of controlling light. (Courtesy General Electric
Company, Large Lamp Department.)

SOURCE AT CENTER

Figure 3–2   Spherical mirror. (Courtesy General Electric Company, Large
Lamp Department.)

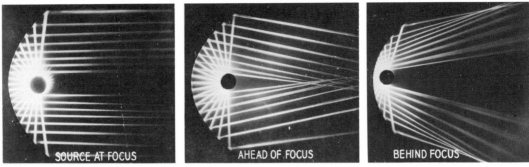

Figure 3–3   Parabolic reflectors. (Courtesy General Electric Company, Large Lamp Department.)

by an interior black paint that would completely absorb the illumination from the lamp that did not fall on the reflector and lens. The available black paint reflects a small part of the incident light and it comes through the lens outside of the desired beam and becomes spill light or stray light, many times falling on the wrong place.

Clear materials and translucent materials are said to transmit light or allow light to pass through them. Clear materials allow

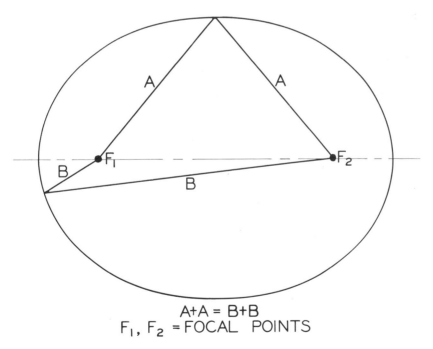

$$A+A = B+B$$
$$F_1, F_2 = FOCAL \ POINTS$$

Figure 3–4   Ellipsoidal reflector diagram. (Courtesy General Electric Company, Large Lamp Department.)

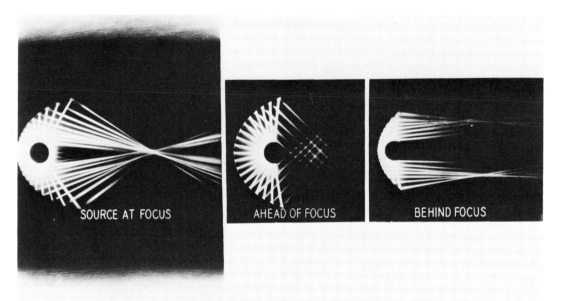

Figure 3–5 Ellipsoidal reflectors. (Courtesy General Electric Company, Large Lamp Department.)

light to pass through them with very little change in direction, but they all absorb a small part of the light and, depending on the angle, tend to reflect some of the light from the surface.

Translucent materials that one cannot see through but that transmit light, such as milk white glass, etched, or sand-blasted glass, and

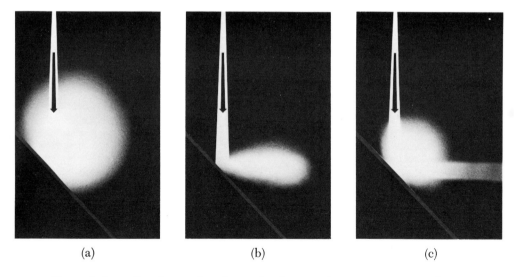

(a)   (b)   (c)

Figure 3–6 Diffused spread and mixed reflection. (Courtesy General Electric Company, Large Lamp Department.)

some ceramic materials, diffuse or spread the beam and scatter it. This is useful in inside-frost incandescent lamps and in luminares that conceal the lamp and reduce surface brightness and glare.

When a ray of light falls on a piece of plate glass (parallel sides) at an angle other than 90°, the ray is bent slightly toward the normal (perpendicular). The glass, being denser than air, causes the ray to bend this way. When the ray leaves the glass, it is bent away from the normal and enters the air again, parallel to its original direction. When the sides are not parallel, as in a glass prism or lens, the ray other than the perpendicular is bent twice in the same direction. In the case shown in Figure 4–4, a plano-convex lens, the bending of the rays is toward the center or perpendicular axis and forms a converging lens. Further discussion of lenses and reflectors for spotlights will be found in Chapter 4 in the section on conventional lens spotlights.

A triangular glass prism might be thought of as a portion of a plano-convex lens. Or stating it in reverse, a plano-convex lens might be composed of several prisms. When a beam of light is passed through a prism the light is "broken up" and emitted as a rainbow of colors—violet, blue, green, yellow, orange and red (see Chapter 5).

These few remarks on the basic concepts of light and illumination should help the reader to understand the behavior of light in the various instruments or luminares discussed in Chapter 4.

LIGHTING
INSTRUMENTS

CHAPTER 4

INTRODUCTION

"These are changing times" has become a cliché but it is true, indeed, concerning lighting equipment in the theatre. Lighting instruments remained almost unchanged for about 25 years. Now the outlook is optimistic for better instrumentation, but we still must be shrewd buyers to avoid the obsolete. Fortunately for the directors and technical directors of college, school, and community theatres, ethical standards in salesmanship have improved in the last 25 years. Most of the representatives of lighting equipment manufacturers are college graduates with considerable experience in lighting plays. In other words, they speak our language, and they help architects and engineers with specifications for new theatres, being genuinely helpful to workers in the nonprofessional theatre. Then too, there are available a number of theatre and stage lighting consultants with possibly less bias in writing specifications for competitive bidding.

Catalogs, too, have greatly improved, with better photographs, diagrams, and useful data to help us make better selections. Committees of the Illuminating Engineering Society have been influential in persuading manufacturers to publish more complete and unbiased information about their equipment. There is still more to be done, however. For example, it would be highly desirable from our point of view to have the efficiency, or the actual amount of light as measured by an independent testing laboratory, stated under each instrument in the lighting catalog. No doubt it will take some time to persuade all of the manufacturers to do this. Since the salesman and the catalog will continue to present a somewhat prejudiced point of view, the people who actually use this equipment day in and day out should make the final selection. Training, actual experience with lighting equipment, and shrewd purchasing ability are still needed, and the only substitute for these essentials is authoritative and unbiased technical advice. Because one manufacturer makes the best spotlights, it does not follow that his floodlights are equally good. Accordingly, the purpose of this chapter is to show how to prevent this kind of mistake and to discuss the best that is available, so that directors and technical workers will be able to select lighting instruments more intelligently and handle them more effectively.

For the past several years the manufacturers of stage lighting instruments have been concerned with the development of a new incandescent lamp (see page 69). The tungsten halogen lamp is a much more compact, efficient, and longer-lived light source that could not be ignored by manufacturers and users of lighting equipment. Many instruments have been redesigned for the smaller source, and in other cases existing designs have been adapted by changing reflectors and other details. In some cases the "jacketed" halogen lamps have been made to fit existing instrument designs. Changes due to the new lamp continue, and some radical changes are being promised. Indeed, the lamps themselves are rapidly undergoing changes and improvements.

This chapter presents the requirements and specifications for good lighting instruments, compares the instruments, and suggests a basis for judgment in their selection for various functions. For purposes of discussion we shall classify everything used in stage lighting as (a) instruments, (b) accessories, (c) projection equipment, and (d) control equipment. The first two will be discussed in the present chapter, and the third and fourth will be considered in Chapters 5 and 8. Instruments will be analyzed and explained under these headings: spotlights, striplights, floodlights, special instruments, and accessories.

STANDARDS FOR JUDGMENT

While there is a convenient method of controlling the output of an incandescent lamp by dimming it from the control board, the lighting instrument itself (and its accessories) plays a more important part in the control of light. The quantity and distribution (see p. 3) of light are affected by the size and shape of the whole instrument; the size, shape, material, and reflecting surface of the reflector; and the size, shape, and type of lens, as well as other details mentioned below. The distribution of light from an instrument should be studied more carefully than is possible by taking a quick look at the wattage and price in a catalog. For example, one should know whether a striplight produces a narrow wedge of light or a wide spread; whether color mixing occurs 3 feet from the striplight or 6 feet away. Concerning a floodlight, it is important to know that the distribution is even, not spotty, when cramped circumstances cause the floodlights to be placed 6 feet from the cyclorama instead of 12 feet or more. The angle of spread at a useful distance with different lenses, the evenness over the lighted area, and the spill light beyond the direct beam are important matters in the selection of spotlights. A rough estimate of the distribution can be determined by studying the instrument under actual conditions of use (advisable in any case), but accurate comparisons that tell the whole story for many uses should include an examination of the candle-power distribution curves made by an impartial testing laboratory.

Some catalogs contain much more helpful suggestions than others, such as diameter of lighted areas, distribution curves, total lumen output, foot-candles, and fairly accurate values of efficiency.

Any careful study or comparison of lighting instruments for the stage should also include the following considerations:

Size

Each manufacturer builds his instruments as compactly as possible within the limits of economy, lens size, efficiency, and the lamp sizes he recommends for the specific instrument. He also designs the instrument for sufficient natural ventilation, except in larger sizes in which blowers are built in. The user of the instrument should follow instructions or recommendations concerning the size of the lamp. Some 1000-watt lamps have the same base and light center lengths as a 500-watt lamp, but doubling the recommended wattage will break lenses, shorten the life of the lamp, and make the instrument much too hot to handle without the addition of forced ventilation.

Ventilation

The better instrument manufacturers provide for a minimum amount of ventilation for the lamp wattage they recommend. The better instruments have holes and slots with proper baffling to control light leaks while allowing sufficient cool air to enter below and hot air to escape above. Instruments for lamps larger than 2000 watts are usually provided with electric blowers, but blowers are frequently too noisy for dramatic productions.

Weight vs. Durability

Lightness is certainly a desirable quality in a lighting instrument if no sacrifice need be made in strength, rigidity, and long life. Most instruments, however, are subjected to rough treatment and careless handling, and so require rugged construction. From catalog pictures it is sometimes difficult to see why similar spotlights should be as different in price as $60 compared with $90. On close comparison of the actual instruments it will be obvious that the construction of one is so far superior to the other that, in a television studio, the one costing 50 percent more will last four times as long. The cheaper one may, on the other hand, be entirely satisfactory in a college theatre producing six plays a year.

Efficiency

The efficiency of a lighting instrument cannot be determined without an illumination meter. Efficiency, as the term is used here, means the amount of light emitted from the instrument divided by the amount of light emitted from the lamp. Striplights and floodlights are nearly always more efficient than spotlights, and in any one type of instrument efficiencies will be found that vary from 5 to 30 percent. When one is purchasing a considerable number of lighting instruments, it is well to have efficiency tests on instruments of different manufacturers made by an impartial testing laboratory. A general idea of efficiencies of each type of instrument will appear in the detailed discussion of that instrument.

Adaptability

For those community theatre workers who own only a few instruments, those with the highest degree of adaptability for several purposes are best. For example, a certain spotlight might be useful as a beam spotlight, a bridge or teaser spotlight, or for lens projections, but in making it adaptable something might be sacrificed that would limit its usefulness for any one of these purposes. A very good striplight, however, can be made to serve equally well as a teaser or border striplight, footlights, or for cyclorama base lighting.

Standardization

It is well, in planning and accumulating equipment over a period of years, to select items that have interchangeable parts, easily replaced parts, and a minimum number of different sizes in accessories such as lenses, screws, bolts, color frames, and lamp sizes and bases. The use of one standard size of stage connectors will save endless hours of interchanging and will reduce the number of connectors and cable that must be kept in stock. On the other hand, it is nearly impossible to standardize to any great extent when one buys a few instruments each year and wants to keep up with improvements as they are developed.

Price

Good lighting equipment certainly is not cheap, but as in many other markets, money cannot be saved by buying poor equipment that is inefficient, obsolete, or poorly constructed and frequently out of service when needed. Manufacturers and dealers give small discounts to educational institutions. When inquiring about prices one should mention discounts to schools.

Specifications

In equipping a new or rebuilt theatre, when a large number of instruments is to be purchased, careful specifications must be written. This is particularly essential if many bidders are concerned. The theatre personnel may mention a well-known manufacturer, but a state purchasing agency may insist on "or equivalent" being written into the specifications. Equivalency is very difficult to prove either way. The only safe way of being certain of getting what one wants is to write extremely tight specifications, specifying every aspect of an instrument down to the smallest detail, even the gauge of the sheet metal. Such specifications take a lot of time to prepare —but they save many regrets later. It is very hard to prove that the cheaper equipment is not "just as good" unless the specifications are complete and detailed.

CONVENTIONAL LENS SPOTLIGHTS

The housing of a conventional spotlight can be of sheet metal properly reinforced for strength and rigidity, or it can be a metal casting. In either case it must be durable and well ventilated, with a length suited to the longest focal-length lens needed. Its diameter is determined by the diameter of the lens and the height of the lamp intended for this instrument. The access door is now usually in front, although a few spotlights open in the rear and have a method of shifting the reflector to remove the lamp.

Figure 4–1   Century Strand Fresnel lens spotlight.

Figure 4–2   Kliegl 8-inch Fresnel lens spotlight.

Figure 4–3   Strand Electric 8-inch Fresnel lens spotlight. (Photo courtesy R. W. Sheppard.)

Since the cost of spotlights is already high, custom building would be out of the question. One needs to compromise and accept one or two undesirable features in order to get the best combination. Twenty-five percent more light from a spotlight justifies having an access door in the wrong place.

The focusing slide, lamp socket, and reflector should be a unit assembly which will slide easily within the hood and which can be quickly and easily held in any position. Strips of metal that move with this assembly should be placed under the socket to prevent light from spilling through the slot in the bottom of the hood.

There are at least two improvements in this method of moving the lamp back and forth. One is a spiral screw controlled by a crank at the rear. The other is a simple lever mechanism with a calibrated scale on the front and the rear of the instrument, allowing the operator to record the position of the lamp for a more accurate change in focus from scene to scene. Each of these is good, but adds considerably to the cost of the spotlight. The old method is still satisfactory.

Reflectors

The light that falls on the lens is actually a very small part of the total output of a spotlight lamp; so a spherical reflector is mounted directly behind the lamp socket, mentioned above, to increase the efficiency about 40 percent. This reflector must have a regular reflect-

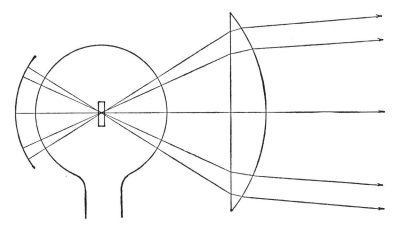

Figure 4–4   Plano-convex lens and spherical reflector.

ing surface, such as polished aluminum,[1] so that light falling upon
it will return directly to the center of curvature of the reflector,
which should be at the center of the lamp filament. If the reflector
mounting is designed and set by the manufacturer to prevent any
misplacement when it is returned to the spotlight after necessary
removal (for dusting or relamping), many irregularities in the
distribution of light will be avoided (see Figure 4–4).

The spherical reflector has undergone some slight change when
used with the new halogen lamps. The double-ended single-
contact lamp required a "socket" at the edges of the reflector.
The "jacketed" halogen lamps can be used in the older conventional spotlights if the "light center length" of the new lamp is
the same as that of the older tungsten lamp intended for this
spotlight.

Lenses

A lens is a piece of glass or other transparent material shaped in
such a way that it will bend or refract a ray of light passing through
it. Unlike window glass, a lens must have nonparallel surfaces.
While some lenses are thinner in the center than they are near the
outer edge, most lenses used in stage lighting instruments are
thicker in the center. These are called *converging lenses*, that is,
lenses that bend the rays of light into a beam or cone of light. Most
converging lenses are either double convex or plano-convex. The

---

[1] Alzak, a patented process, is the best known method of treating aluminum
for long wear and a high reflecting surface.

first has two curved sides and the second has one plane side and one curved side (Figure 4–4). The curved surfaces are portions of a sphere; the plano-convex lens might have been sliced from a glass ball.

Each lens is said to have a focal point to which parallel rays of light converge after passing through the lens. Theoretically, if a source of light were placed at this focal point, the rays of light, after passing through the lens, would continue in parallel lines. The focal length of a lens is the distance from the focal point to a point within the lens. Notice the line drawn through the middle of a lens perpendicular to the plane face in Figure 4–4. This is called the optical axis, and will serve as a convenient base line on which to study optical images and along which to make measurements and calculations. If a bright object is placed beyond the focal point above the optical axis of a converging lens, an image of this object will appear on the opposite side of the lens, below the axis and upside down.

Such a condition would be undesirable in a spotlight, since this image might fall on the scenery or on an actor's face. If a spotlight were designed for a specific lens, the slot or other focusing device would not allow the filament of the lamp to reach the focal point, and at the other end would not allow the lamp to touch the lens. Three-eighths of an inch clearance is usually allowed to prevent cracking the lens or melting the bulb of the lamp if the two come too close to each other. Within this focal range, a good spotlight will produce a narrow beam by pulling the lamp assembly (reflector and lamp) to the rear of the hood, and when the lamp is near the lens a sufficiently wide spread of light should result. The most useful diameters in spotlight lenses (plano-convex) are 4½ inches, 6 inches, and 8 inches. Useful focal lengths vary with the diameter, but it is desirable to have a short focal length to increase the efficiency of a spotlight (explained below) even though this requires thicker glass, is more expensive, and provides more uneven illumination.

To solve the problem of excessively thick glass, the Fresnel-type lens was developed for spotlights (see Figure 4–5). The concentric ribs, or steps, are elements of lenses of nearly the same focal length but of different diameters, cast from heat-resistant glass in one flat disc. As mentioned above, the concentric ribs tend to make shadow rings in the light beam, and so require a diffusing (not completely, of course) pattern on the back of the lens. For any given diameter the focal lengths can be much shorter [8 × 5 (8-inch diameter, 5-inch focal length) Fresnel instead of 8 × 10 plano-convex], allowing the filament to be nearer the lens, and thus increasing the

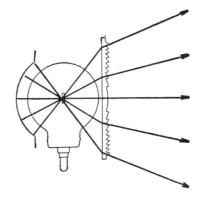

Figure 4–5 Fresnel lens and spherical reflector. (Courtesy Century Strand, Inc.)

efficiency with a relatively narrow beam of light and no chromatic aberration (color bands in the beam). These flat Fresnel lenses are vary satisfactory for the stage under circumstances where the "soft edge" spill light outside the center of the beam is not objectionable. They are very satisfactory for "first pipe" batten[2] mounting for stage area lighting when the walls of the set tend to control the spill light. Sometimes funnels and barn doors are used to cut part of the spill. In space-stage lighting (see Chapter 9), where every possible trace of spill light must be eliminated, plano-convex lenses are always used and funnels are added to the spotlights. The flat Fresnel lens is never used for balcony front and ceiling port positions because the spill light would be excessive on walls and proscenium arch. In ellipsoidal spotlights a concavo-convex Fresnel lens or a flat Fresnel lens with no diffusing pattern is used interchangeably with the plano-convex lens either to make possible a lens of slightly smaller focal length, or to save money. Spill light is a little more noticeable with this lens than with the plano-convex. See end of this section for ellipsoidal spotlights.

Lens and Spotlight Efficiency

One can see from Figures 4–4 and 4–5 that the basic problem of spotlight efficiency (output divided by input), or getting the most out of a conventional spotlight, is rather simple. The closer the lamp is to the lens opening, the larger the solid angle of light. This solid angle is a cone with the filament at the apex; the base of the cone is the opening for the lens. It is obvious that the angle in Figure 4–5 is greater than in Figure 4–4. Stated another way, that lens which

---

[2] First pipe means a suspended pipe batten just upstage from the teaser. Outlets are distributed along its length where instruments may be connected.

allows the lamp to be nearest to it will produce the greatest amount of light on a specific area. Any lens will allow proximity of the lamp, but some lenses will spread the light so far that it is no longer useful in lighting a specific area. In a general way, then, the best lens is the one that produces a fairly narrow beam with the lamp as close to the lens as possible. Since moving the lamp away from the lens (to produce a narrow beam) loses light, the better approach is to move the focal point of the lens toward the filament. This, of course, is leading to the shortest workable focal length for any given diameter. Obviously, the largest practicable diameter will increase the amount of light, too. Actually, efficiency is concerned with the ratio of the diameter to the focal length. Theoretically, an 8×5 lens should produce twice as much light as an 8×10 lens. Furthermore, since the ratio of 8 to 12 is the same as that of 6 to 9, a lens with an 8-inch diameter and 12-inch focal length should have, theoretically, the same efficiency as a lens with a 6-inch diameter and 9-inch focal length. The following explanation of the graph in Figure 4–6 should help to understand spotlight lenses better, and

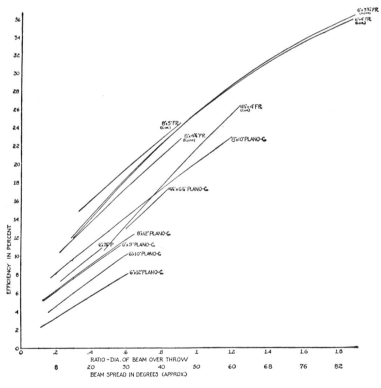

Figure 4–6   Showing efficiency of spotlights with lenses of different focal lengths and different diameters.

perhaps help to select the best one to use under various circumstances, from both the theoretical and practical points of view.

The graph in Figure 4–6 was made to compare the efficiency of lenses of various diameters and focal lengths. Both plano-convex and Fresnel lenses were studied, and many thousands of readings were taken with voltmeters and illumination meters to obtain the data from which these curves were drawn. Most of the curves for the plano-convex lenses are short and approach a straight line because the lamps used were of the G (spherical) type and would not allow the filament to go closer to the lens. The curve for the 8-inch diameter and 10-inch focal length was extended by adding readings taken with a T (tubular) lamp that could be placed somewhat closer to the lens. These additional data were added when this study was continued to include Fresnel lenses whose focal lengths are so short that one must use lamps that can be placed nearer to the lens. These points, at the extreme right in any of the curves corresponding to beam spreads of 60° or more, are of academic interest only, because an extreme flood focus in a spotlight is rarely useful. In fact, one can be deceived very easily by the manufacturer of a spotlight with a 6-inch diameter Fresnel lens who says that his spotlight has an efficiency of over 35 percent. As one can see from the two curves extending into the upper right-hand corner, his claim is true; but look down below at the spread of the beam—over 80°, more of a flood than a spot. The graph's usefulness lies in comparing lenses in this way. Take some reasonable spread of light for a spotlight, such as 20°, follow up from the lens of lowest efficiency, the 6 × 12, to the highest, the 8 × 5 Fresnel. Logically, the 8 × 4¾ Fresnel curve should be almost superimposed on the 8 × 5, like the two 6-inch Fresnel curves that lie between the two 8-inch lens curves. One possible explanation for the deviation from the expected results in the case of the 8 × 4¾ Fresnel is this: All Fresnel lenses[3] have a diffusing pattern on the back that prevents circular shadows in the lighted area, particularly at short throws. Considerable amounts of stray light that are hard to measure are caused by this diffusing pattern, and some lenses have more of it than others.

Some practical considerations, too, come into the selection of lenses. An old rule of thumb that can be followed is to use a short focal length for a short throw and a long focal length for a long throw. This rule is satisfactory if one understands its meaning and uses, according to the curves in the graph (Figure 4–6), the shortest

---

[3] Referring to those used in conventional spotlights.

focal length for any given diameter of lens that will produce an even distribution of light without chromatic aberration (irregular color bands in the lighted area). For example, one might want to use an 8-inch-diameter lens spotlight on the first pipe (or bridge) part of the time, and at other times move it out front to a ceiling port or beam position, where the distance to the stage is probably three times as great as that from light bridge[4] to stage. At the shorter throw one could use a 10-inch focal length and produce a 35° beam spread for ordinary area lighting. From the curve one can see that the efficiency is nearly 16 percent. For another play this spotlight might be needed out front, perhaps 50 feet away from the stage. Now, in order to have about the same size lighted area on the stage, the beam spread has to be cut to 8°. But to make the beam narrower, the lamp must be moved further back in the spotlight. Referring again to the curve opposite 8°, one finds the efficiency reduced to 8 percent, that is, cut in half. But now there is more trouble. In trying to get a narrow beam with this lens, the lamp was moved too near the focal point and there is a lot of chromatic aberration—another unsatisfactory, uneven beam of light. There is nothing else to do but to change the lens to one of longer focal length—the 8 × 12. We can see from the graph that our efficiency has dropped to nearly 6 percent, a 25 percent loss of light, but we have gained a more even beam of light that will enhance the appearance of the actor and his costume. To regain the lost light we change the size of the lamp to 1500 watts instead of the usual 1000 watts, if our circuit will allow it. This is a good example of increasing the adaptability of a spotlight by changing the lens.

Mounting

All spotlights are equipped with a yoke for mounting on a floor stand or on a pipe batten. Ordinarily, the yoke can be attached to the vertical pipe of the floor stand with a machine screw instead of a "C" clamp. The "C" clamp shown in Figure 4–1 is the most common method of connecting the spotlight yoke to a horizontal pipe batten. Some manufacturers make adapters for mounting spotlights or other instruments on vertical pipes such as tormentor battens or "trees."

[4] A steel frame with a narrow walkway and battens with outlets, suspended by sets of lines from the gridiron, is a better device for mounting area spotlights. Two pipe battens, one above the other, provided with electrical outlets, usually form the upstage side of a bridge (Figure 4–7).

Figure 4–7 Lighting bridge hung from gridiron near teaser. View from stage looking into auditorium. (Courtesy California State University, San Diego, Audio-Visual Services.)

Color Frame Guides

Adequate guides for color frames are provided on the front of all spotlights for the theatre. The type that is closed on three sides and open at the top is preferred by some technicians because the type made in three pieces might allow a careless operator to miss the bottom piece and allow the color frame to fall and injure a person below.

Range of Sizes

Several manufacturers make a complete line of Fresnel lens spotlights from the 3-inch lens size (100 watts or 150 watts) up to ones with a 14-inch lens and a lamp as large as 5000 watts if desired (primarily for television). The 6-inch lens size for a 500-watt T20 lamp makes a good upstage instrument for mounting on a bridge or first pipe on a small stage. For larger stages the 8-inch lens, 1000-to-2000-watt instrument is recommended for a similar purpose. The 3-inch Fresnel lens instrument is best for restricted mounting places, hiding behind properties or other small objects, or screwing to the back side of scenery.

New Designs

Many spotlights have been redesigned for the new tungsten halogen lamps discussed on p. 69. Since many of these lamps are small in diameter (about ½ inch, depending on wattage) and have contacts at both ends, the reflectors of the spotlights in particular had to be modified to accept this new lamp. For the use of owners of older models of spotlights, lamp manufacturers have made tungsten halogen lamps with the older bases (see Figures 4–23 and 4–24).

In the last few years at least two manufacturers have made a conventional Fresnel lens spotlight (in several sizes) with a new reflector shape (at least partly ellipsoidal) and a different type of tungsten halogen lamp. They claim an efficiency of as high as 60 percent compared 10 to 15 percent with older models. This is hardly a fair comparison, because the 60-percent figure was obtained at flood focus, not a practical lamp position. See Figures 4–4 and 4–5.

ELLIPSOIDAL SPOTLIGHTS

Except for the change in conventional spotlights mentioned in the paragraph above, the ellipsoidal spotlight represents one of the few radical changes in spotlight design since the nineteenth century. The ellipsoidal spotlight, named for its reflector shape, first appeared in the mid-1930's and has become our most important and useful acting area instrument. The selection of an ellipsoidal shape for a spotlight reflector may have evolved from a desire to find a way to use all of that wasted light that is absorbed by the black paint in a conventional spotlight. Another glance at Figures 4–4 and 4–5 will remind one of the enormous loss of light between the small solid angles subtended by the reflector and the lens. The ellipsoid subtends a much greater solid angle of light.

Figure 4–8 shows a ray diagram of an ellipse, or more accurately, about one-half of an ellipse (see Figures 3–4 and 3–5). If the curved shape at the left were continued symmetrically around to the right we would have a complete ellipse. The proportions of an

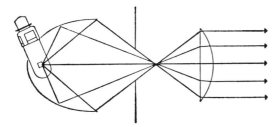

Figure 4–8 Ray diagram of ellipsoidal spotlight. (Courtesy Century Strand, Inc.)

ellipse can vary according to the relative lengths of its vertical and horizontal axes. In other words, one could design a long skinny ellipse or a short fat ellipse, of which the circle would be a special case. The two focal points of this figure are shown on the horizontal axis; the first focal point is at the center of the lamp filament and the second one is where the light rays cross at the right. In fact, all rays emanating from a light source at the first focal point (left in Figure 4–8) that fall anywhere on the reflector are redirected to the second focal point. If we rotate the ellipse around its horizontal axis it becomes a solid three-dimensional figure, the ellipsoid.

The manufacturers of ellipsoidal spotlights have learned that about one-half of an ellipsoid is all that is useful and practical in spotlight design. Increasing the diameter of the lens system would not justify increases in cost and weight for a small increase in efficiency. The inside surface of the ellipsoid is a highly polished regular or specular reflecting surface, "flatted" or broken up slightly so that the reflected rays will fill a hole in a metal plate called the *gate*. If lamp filaments were the size of a theoretical point and there were no large hole in the rear of the reflector to make a dark area in the beam of light, there might be possible a more precise and efficient optical system in an ellipsoidal spotlight. While the direct unreflected light from the lamp is only a small part of the total light, much of it is absorbed in the black paint around the gate, and the little that goes through the gate to the lens system is not well integrated with the reflected part of the light. The "flatted" pattern on the reflector helps to tie all the irregularities together: the filament size, the direct emanation, and the loss of reflector surface in the hole for the lamp. Thus the gate opening is filled with a fairly even distribution of light. The gate opening is near the second focal point of the ellipsoid where the reflected rays cross.

The lens or lens system can be a single plano-convex lens, a pair of plano-convex lenses to provide a shorter focal length, or a "step"

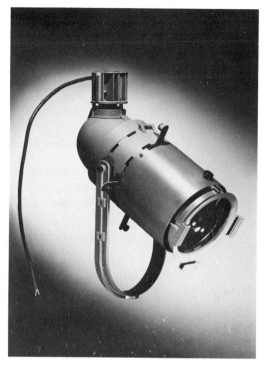

Figure 4–9   Kliegl 3-inch lens ellipsoidal spotlight.

Figure 4–10   Century Strand 6-inch ellipsoidal spotlight.

lens.[5] The step lens is a relative of the Fresnel lens without the diffusing pattern on the back. Some step lenses are flat and others are concavo-convex. The better ones are provided with black ceramic risers (between the steps). Black risers tend to reduce the spill light, which is somewhat worse in step lenses than it is in plano-convex lenses. It is important to notice at this point that the optical system in the ellipsoidal spotlight is entirely different from the simple convergence of light from a filament through a condenser. In the ellipsoidal spotlight the lens or lens combination, although crude and uncorrected, behaves like an objective or projection lens as it is aligned in this instrument. The whole instrument is a lens projector in principle, as much as any of those described in Chapter 5. The gate corresponds to a slide holder and the lighted area on the stage is the image reversed, as are all images in lens projectors. Ellipsoidal

[5] Mr. John Hoxie of the Corning Glass Co. has suggested to me that we should refer to lenses of this type in ellipsoidal spotlights as step lenses and to those in conventional spotlights as Fresnel lenses to avoid confusion. They are similar in pattern.

spotlights are provided with an adjustment screw that allows the lens-holding cylinder to be moved in or out an inch or so to sharpen or soften the edges of the image (beam on area). Two methods of adjusting the size and shape of the image are also available. These instruments can be purchased with an iris fastened against the gate to adjust the diameter of a circular area, but a more common beam-shape controller is a set of four framing shutters. Each can be moved to make the beam smaller or larger, square, rectangular, and with nonparallel sides. Some of these instruments have a slot at the gate where simple patterns of metal or other heat-resisting materials may be placed to project such images to the stage. Since the lenses are not of projection lens quality, simple patterns are preferred. Stylized foliage patterns punched from sheet metal (supplemented with a green color medium) are often seen. Although the lenses are of the quality of condensers, they must be heat resisting. The focal length of lenses or lens systems must be shorter than the distance from the gate to the nearest lens; otherwise there will be no projected image on the stage.

Ellipsoidal spotlights, manufactured in many sizes and shapes, are usually designated by their lens diameter, which may vary from 3 inches to 10 inches, with some even larger. All are made to take the new tungsten halogen lamp (see p. 69), the smaller ones for 400- or 500-watt lamps and the larger ones for 1000- or 1500-watt lamps (see Figures 4–9 through 4–12). One should study the catalog data to select the ellipsoidal instrument with a beam spread best suited to the distance at which the instrument will be used most often. It is highly inefficient to buy a wide-beam spotlight and use it most often with the framing shutters pushed in to half efficiency. At best they are from 20 to 30 percent efficient. Why lose half of it and be back in the old class of conventional spotlights, ca. 1930? One should notice in general that although there are wider beams with a smaller lens diameter, the 3-inch and the 6-inch lens instruments may be purchased with either a narrow beam or a wide-beam lens system. The efficiency is considerably reduced in instruments with the narrower beam. To repeat, this ellipsoidal spotlight is our most generally useful and efficient acting area instrument. It takes a little more mounting space and its shadows are a little harsher than in the case of the Fresnel spotlight. On the other hand, the spill light of the Fresnel is difficult to control. The ellipsoidal spotlight is the only useful one for a long throw and for the anteproscenium positions where spill must be reduced to the absolute minimum. In many cases the ellipsoidal replaces the Fresnel on the bridge or first pipe and in many other locations.

Figure 4–11   Kliegl 1000-watt ellipsoidal spotlight with 10-inch lens diameter.

Figure 4–12   Rank Strand Electric ellipsoidal spotlight. (Photo courtesy R. W. Sheppard.)

FOLLOW SPOTLIGHTS

A follow spotlight is essentially a high-powered instrument either incandescent or arc that will produce a narrow beam of light, a small area at a long throw, a long throw meaning a distance of 100 to 300 feet. Such an instrument might be satisfactory for lighting an outdoor stage from the rear of the auditorium. Many large ellipsoidal spotlights with blowers and lamps of 2000 to 5000 watts have served this purpose rigidly clamped to a batten, but without some modifications they are rather crude as follow spotlights. Preferably, a true follow spotlight should have a firm base and well-balanced vertical and horizontal adjustments so that all of the traditional maneuvers of this type of instrument can be accomplished by a single operator. Furthermore, simple convenient manual controls are needed to change colors, move the lens or lenses, open and close the iris and the top and bottom beam shutters. The direct current arc type shown in Figure 4–13 is quite long but well-balanced, with all the controls centrally located. The rectifier that changes alternating current to direct is in the base, and the upper rear section contains the carbons and their reflector. After the arc is struck (carbons pushed together), the carbons maintain the correct distance automatically. They do burn up now and then, and the operator must plan his changes for a convenient time (intermissions hopefully), not in the middle of a song he is following.

Figure 4–13   Strong Electric follow spotlight.

Follow spotlights are rarely used for dramatic production, but it is conceivable that one or more might be called for in a "far out" contemporary entertainment. They are, however, traditional and rarely omitted from musicals and musical reviews. When a singer or singers are doing a number the operator is expected to follow them about the stage, adjusting the diameter of the beam to suit their positions. If they separate, another follow spotlight must pick up one of the singers so that they have equal emphasis. When the number is over, the operator must "iris out" (close the iris), because the arc cannot be dimmed. At times when the arc is on, the general area is dimmed part way down for greater contrast. The arc follow spotlight (or two) is also used for dance concerts to follow solo performances and leading dancers.

PARALLEL BEAM PROJECTORS

The parallel beam projector instrument is primarily a parabolic reflector from 8 to 16 inches in diameter (even larger for outdoor lighting) built into a housing with an appropriate lamp socket and accessories for controlling direct emanation. Like the elliptical shape mentioned above, the parabola is designed by means of an algebraic formula. With different values in the formula the parabola may be shallow or deep. A shallow parabolic shape is customarily employed in the parallel beam projector (see Figure 4–14). If a theoretical point source of light is placed on the focal point of this shape, all reflected rays leave the polished (regular reflecting) surface of the reflector in straight lines. The three-dimensional figure is produced by rotating the plane figure around its horizontal axis. Even though a concentrated filament is not a theoretical point, the light rays leave the polished surface essentially in straight lines. On the other hand, there is a considerable amount of direct emanation from the lamp that does not fall on the reflector but must be controlled. This is done in two ways. In one type there is a small spherical reflector in front of the lamp that sends the light back through the filament to the parabolic reflector; in others a black cylinder (or concentric cylinders) is placed in front of the lamp to absorb the direct emanation. See the examples in Figures 4–14 and 4–15. A useful size is about 14 inches in diameter with a socket for a 1500- or 2000-watt lamp. Three or four of these might be an important part of the inventory of a medium-size theatre to serve as sidelighting in exteriors, moonlight, and sunlight. While ellipsoidal spotlights serve such a purpose, the parallel beam projector is considerably more efficient. It can be purchased with a "focusing" device to spread the beam when needed.

Figure 4–14 Century Strand parallel beam projector.

Figure 4–15 Kliegl 1000-to-2000-watt parallel beam projector.

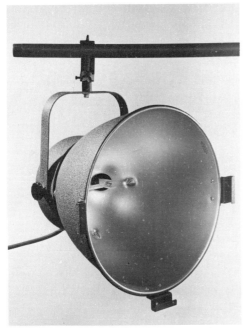

Figure 4–16   Kliegl   500-to-1000-watt "scoop" floodlight. This takes a variety of halogen cycle lamps.

Figure 4–17   Century Strand ellipsoidal floodlight.

FLOODLIGHTS

The old box-type floodlight is now obsolete. While a few of these are still in use, floodlights that are more efficient, lighter, more easily mounted, and more suitable in light distribution to the needs of modern stage lighting are now preferred by technical workers in all theatres. Figures 4–16 and 4–17 illustrate two of the best, each of which consists of a spun-aluminum reflector with a diffuse reflecting surface (guides for a color frame to drop in at the top should be added for the theatre), a mogul receptacle, and a small yoke with pipe clamp. The shape of this reflector is ellipsoidal (see discussion of ellipsoidal spotlights above); but a parabolic reflector is also common and equally good. When floodlights are mounted above on battens to light the cyclorama or perhaps a drop, cramped stage conditions may demand that the floodlight batten be 4 or 5 feet from the surface to be illuminated. Under such conditions, the ellipsoidal shape will probably produce a smoother distribution. The 500-watt size has the advantage of taking less space in mounting and is of ample intensity for college and community theatres.

A floodlight produces general illumination similar to the distribution of only one unit in a striplight; by the same token, the illumination from a whole row of floodlights is similar to the distribution of one striplight, but probably greater in spread. Floodlights can be used interchangeably with striplights in some cases, one taking the place of a short strip for illuminating backings, several replacing a borderlight to provide the general illumination for the acting area, or most important of all, a number of them, on a batten, lighting the cyclorama from above. In this case they are more satisfactory than any other instrument for this purpose. In some cases they are mounted close together in rows on a pipe batten and connected in two circuits, one light blue and one dark blue, for changes from day to night scenes. Perhaps even better than a single batten mounting for cyclorama lighting would be a rectangular pipe frame of several short battens, supporting a large number of floodlights. This frame is hung 15 or 20 feet from the cyclorama to produce a more even distribution of light over the surface than that produced by a single, longer row placed closer to the cyclorama. These floodlights are exceedingly useful instruments for many purposes.

STRIPLIGHTS

Striplight is used here as a general term that includes borderlights, footlights, cyclorama border or footlights, and backing striplights. Older striplights (now obsolete) consisted of an open painted trough, with sockets and wiring compartment below.

One of the two best types of striplight units (Figure 4–18) consists of a row of individual reflectors, each containing one lamp and a round glass color medium that completely covers the mouth of the reflector. The reflector should be of Alzak aluminum, with either a specular (polished) or a diffuse reflecting surface. Alzak has a reflectance[6] of at least 80 percent. The diffuse surface tends to spread the light a little more than the polished surface. The shape of the reflector is a combination of parabolic and spherical, which seems to produce the best distribution in striplights. The reflector with a parabolic shape tends to send out light in straight lines if the source is placed at the focus. A spherical reflector was explained above (see p. 47) and the ray diagram in Figures 2–5 and 4–4. Striplights should be wired in three or four circuits for the three primary colors, blue green, and red (see Chapter 5), and possibly one for white light. The color roundel, which is placed in the mouth of the reflector, is of heavy heat-resistant glass that is not

---

[6] The reflectance is the amount of light reflected from a surface divided by the light falling on that surface. It is usually expressed in percent.

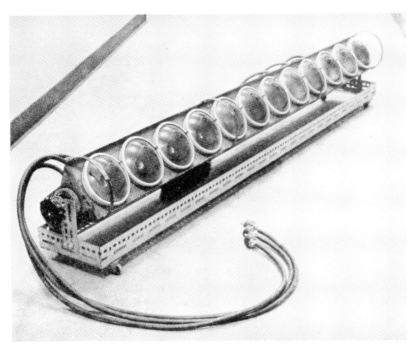

Figure 4–18   Three-color reflector striplight section (Major) in punched-steel angle iron frame for use as cyclorama footlights.

easily broken in normal use. These color media are readily inter-changeable. Reputable dealers carry five or six colors in stock. Varia-tions in distribution are possible by changing the reflector surface (an expensive process), lamp, and color roundel. For a sharp, narrow wedge of light, when the surface to be illuminated is at a considerable distance, the specular (polished) reflector, clear lamp, and clear roundel might be indicated. For the maximum spread at close range, one can use the diffuse reflector, inside frost lamp, and the diffusing color roundels. Various other combinations of the three may give better results under special circumstances.

The second satisfactory type of striplight came into common use with the development of the PAR 38 and R40 150-watt spot- and floodlamps (see p. 70). Since these lamps have built-in reflectors, the reflectors mentioned above for the first type of striplight are omitted in this one. This second type (Figure 4–19) consists of the wiring channel, with screw sockets for the lamps, and a sheet-metal housing to protect the lamps and secure the color roundels. Associated with this striplight is a widespread color roundel that allows color mixing near the instrument when it is necessary to place the striplight unusually close to a surface such as the cyclo-rama. Changes in distribution are made possible with this strip-

Figure 4–19   Century Strand striplight for use with R40 lamps.

light by changing from the spot type to the flood type of lamp, or vice versa.

The purpose of striplights, borderlights, and footlights is to produce general illumination; a more wedge-like distribution of light is possible with these two types instead of allowing it to spill over everywhere, as was the case in the earlier models.

Borderlights

A borderlight is just a striplight hanging from an overhead pipe batten to produce general illumination on the acting area from above. Since modern striplights produce a wedge of light, the light can be restricted in part to certain areas. For example, by tipping the borderlight downward, most of the illumination can be kept off the scenery, or any part of the light can be directed to the set by rotating the instrument on its axis. The old method of mounting was by means of chains. More accurate manipulation becomes possible, however, when the instrument is attached by short arms and pipe clamps, one at each end, in a similar manner to the arm-and-clamp method of mounting a spotlight. Borderlights with individual reflectors are made for lamps from 75 to 500 watts; 75 to 150 watts is sufficiently large for the average theatre because the three small sizes, 75, 100, and 150 watts, can be placed on 6-inch centers, and

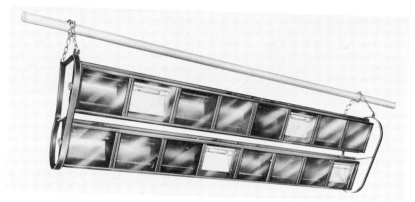

Figure 4–20 Kliegl double-row cyclorama borderlight. Wired for three or four colors and with 300- or 500-watt tungsten halogen lamps.

it is preferable to have like colors near each other to make the distribution as nearly even as possible. An instrument with 150-watt lamps is composed of reflectors on 6-inch centers, while one with 200-watt lamps is on 8-inch centers. There is exactly the same wattage[7] and illumination per foot, but the units of the same color are 6 inches farther apart in the larger one, and the larger one is more expensive—two definite disadvantages.

The latest model in striplight sections is made especially for the tungsten halogen double-ended lamp and is available in various wattages beginning with 300 watts. Since the lamp is more compact than conventional incandescent lamps, the striplight itself can be somewhat more compact. Obviously, striplights can be made in any length and wired with the desired number of circuits (see Figure 4–20).

Before 1930 it was the accepted practice to have several border-lights on a stage, extending from one side of the proscenium arch to the other. In other words, a 36-foot proscenium opening would require a 36-foot borderlight. While these are satisfactory for lighting rehearsals, orchestra, and band practice, striplight sections from 6 to 7½ feet long, with line connectors at one end and load connectors (see p. 75) at the other, are three times as useful (see p. 44). If a section is provided with a studbolt extending from each end, it can be attached to a batten with hangers (Figure 4–19), or set on the floor with feet or carriages with casters (Figure 4–18) for ground row and cyclorama base lighting. These sections are also excellent for direct or indirect footlights.

[7] Total number of watts. See Chapter 7.

Footlights

Footlights usually consist of a striplight concealed from the house by proper recession near the edge of the stage floor outside the curtain line. They should be of very low wattage and need not be longer than three-fourths the width of the proscenium arch. Footlights should be carefully placed to avoid spilling light on the proscenium arch or on the teaser when it is at its lowest useful position. They should not be placed higher than 3½ inches above the stage floor. Like other striplights, they might well be made in 6- or 7½-foot sections, so that less than the full width can be used when desired. Again, like striplights, they should be wired in three circuits for the primary colors. The same colors should not be farther apart than 18 inches so that they will blend well and no spottiness will occur when only one color is in use.

Since the illumination from footlights is directed upwards as well as backstage, large shadows are likely to appear on scenery, because each source of light produces a separate shadow of every object in front of it. This is one of the most objectionable characteristics of ordinary footlights, but the difficulty can be overcome by reversing the striplight to send its illumination in the direction of the audience. To receive this illumination a long trough-like, properly shaped (spherical is a desirable shape) reflector of polished aluminum (with a "broken" or partly diffusing surface) is provided to direct the illumination back to the stage. This reflector acts as a line source of light that does not produce shadows of objects that stand perpendicular to it as the actor does. In this manner, then, indirect footlights solve the problem of annoying footlight shadows.

Most of the epithets hurled at footlights come as a result of their being used as a primary source of light, but this criticism does not apply to footlights of good design that are used for their intended purpose. Color in footlight illumination adds to the general tonality of the setting, but the primary purpose of footlights is to soften facial shadows and to diminish excessive contrasts in the actors' faces caused by illumination from beam spotlights placed in the auditorium ceiling. This function requires illumination of a very low level, and is akin to the function of borderlights and any other source of general illumination—that of blending and reducing contrasts in the distribution of specific illumination from spotlights. One can do very well without footlights if the angle of spotlights in the auditorium ceiling is fairly low, 35° to 40°, except when actors wear broad-brimmed hats. If this angle is about 60°, footlights are necessary in any case. They are, however, more often too bright than too dim.

Backing Striplights

Another type of striplight is cheaper and simpler than the ones discussed above. It, too, is divided into compartments for small-wattage lamps (100 watts or less), but it is wired in only one circuit. This striplight is useful in two, three, or four compartments and serves well, as its name implies, for low-level illumination in small "backing" areas offstage from doors in interior sets. It is useful, also, for corridors, behind archways, and, on occasion, it is placed on the floor between ground rows. There are other ways (R40 lamps or small floods) of lighting a backing, but the backing striplight is rugged and convenient to mount. The hook on one end can be hooked behind a flat in a brace cleat or a screw eye, and it will drop into the end of the pipe on a floor stand.

LIGHTNING AND RAINBOW EFFECTS

A number of effects can be produced, as explained in Chapter 5, by means of lens projections of painted, photographic, or paper-cutout lantern slides. Examples of these are a zigzag cutout made in a piece of black paper for flashes of stylized lightning, tiny holes punched in a tin slide for stars, or a handpainted slide for a rainbow. Such a rainbow effect can be rented or purchased, but anyone familiar with the physics of light can assemble one for temporary use from parts found in almost any department of physics in a college or university. Lightning more naturalistic than that produced by a projected cutout is created by momentary contacts between a carbon and a metal terminal. This lightning effect, which is offered for sale, is properly enclosed to guard against fire. One type is operated by hand, and another is operated by a magnet so that it can be controlled electrically from a distance.

A Linnebach lightning effect (see Chapter 5) can be convincing, too, under the right circumstances. The writer made one for the storm scene in Maxwell Anderson's *High Tor* in the following manner. The basic instrument was an arc floodlight with the white reflecting surface repainted black. The arc carbons rested against each other, and when the switch was closed, the carbons separated, striking the arc. Next, a piece of glass was cut to fit the color frame guides of the arc hood, and painted with a coat of thick black paint of a type that will not flake off. With a photograph as a guide, a forked lightning pattern was scratched with a sharp point through the black paint in a thin line. When the switch was closed momentarily, the movement of the carbon in the striking of the arc gave the projected image on the cyclorama enough movement to make the lightning very dramatic.

Since the development of the electronic flash for photography, the writer has been trying it for lightning on the stage. While this device produces the broad flash of light like the arc, it is at the same time much more convenient, compact, and probably safer. For a broad, open flash, two flashers work better. Some types work on batteries; others plug directly into 120-volt outlets.

A Linnebach rainbow is well suited to a romantic folk play, such as Obey's *Noah*. One can cut a curved slot in a cardboard slide, cover the slot with a piece of transparent plastic, and paint the colored stripes with colored lacquer. KOH-I-NOOR transparent acetate ink, made for painting on plastic materials, is good for this purpose.

FIREPLACE EFFECTS

Fireplaces offer opportunities for variety and beauty in lighting interior settings that are worthy of some consideration. The motivation—that is, the apparent source of light—must be a dimly illuminated, inconspicuous coal grate or set of fire logs, neither of which is difficult to assemble. To produce a coal-grate fire, one can borrow a metal basket and fill it with chunks of amber and black glass. In the bottom of the basket it will be necessary to clamp two receptacles containing lamps of small wattage, which will illuminate the chunks of glass and make them seem like glowing coals. This whole unit can be purchased or borrowed from a department store that uses the grate for window display. Fire logs are expensive to purchase but quite simple and cheap to construct. Taking a board of suitable size and shape as a base, first attach two lamp receptacles, and wire them to illuminate the logs. Then make a form from chicken wire in the shape of the group of logs, coals, and ashes, and attach it to the wooden base. Clearance, of course, must be left to allow the lamps to be placed in the receptacles. The next step is to cover the frame with papier-mâché. Dip strips of newspaper or paper toweling in cold water paste and smoothe it into place over the frame until it is completely covered. When this dries, it forms a durable surface that will stand fairly rough treatment. To complete the logs, punch some holes in appropriate places and cover them with colored cellophane or gelatin, and finally, paint the whole unit to resemble logs. Naturalistic detail is unnecessary, since fire logs are always partly concealed and are never seen at close range. If the fireplace is in a side wall downstage, one or two small spotlights with red and amber color media should be concealed where they can be focused on a chair or sofa to illuminate the actors in this area with the warmth of firelight in contrast, perhaps, to moonlight coming in a window. The amount of illumination from a fireplace should be rather low because of the position and angle of illumination that might produce objectionable shadows on the opposite wall. The ones available for sale are made out of real logs and sell for $30 to $40 from dealers in fireplace accessories.

INCANDESCENT LAMPS

An incandescent lamp consists of a base (the part that screws into the receptacle or socket), which is made in a number of sizes and shapes (Figure 4–21), a bulb of glass of various shapes, the lead-in wires, the filament with different forms, and the filament supports. Lamps with pear-shaped (PS) bulbs are used in floodlights and striplights; lamps with globe-shaped (G) and tubular (T) bulbs are used in spotlights. A small spotlight, such as the 6-inch Fresnel lens instrument, is equipped with a medium prefocus socket for the 250- or 400-watt G lamps and the 500-watt T lamp, each of which is made with a medium prefocus base. As mentioned on p. 46, Figure 4–21 (c) F and M lamps for spotlight service ordinarily have a prefocus base that places the filament in the most efficient position in relationship to the reflector and lens when inserted in the receptacle in the spotlight. Larger lamps for spotlights, such as the 1000 watt with the G or T bulb, are provided with mogul prefocus bases.

Some manufacturers of ellipsoidal spotlights are still using the medium bi-post sockets for 500-, 750- and 1000-watt tungsten halogen lamps. If desired they will provide the medium bi-pin socket.

Lamps for stage lighting instruments are rarely found in catalogs for general service lamps, but nearly all of the common lamps used in spotlights can be found in such catalogs as General Electric's *Lamps for Stage Lighting, Motion Picture and TV Studios*. Some catalogs for stage lighting instruments show recommended lamps for each instrument, and these manufacturers and dealers will provide such lamps. Larger discounts, however, are available through institutional and state lamp contracts.

A new family of incandescent lamps, described as "tungsten halogen," has changed designs of many commercial luminares, including a large number of stage lighting instruments. This lamp could be described as an incandescent tungsten lamp with a halogen regenerative cycle.

The first lamps of this type were made with quartz bulbs, and iodine vapor was used as the regenerative material. Recently, bulbs

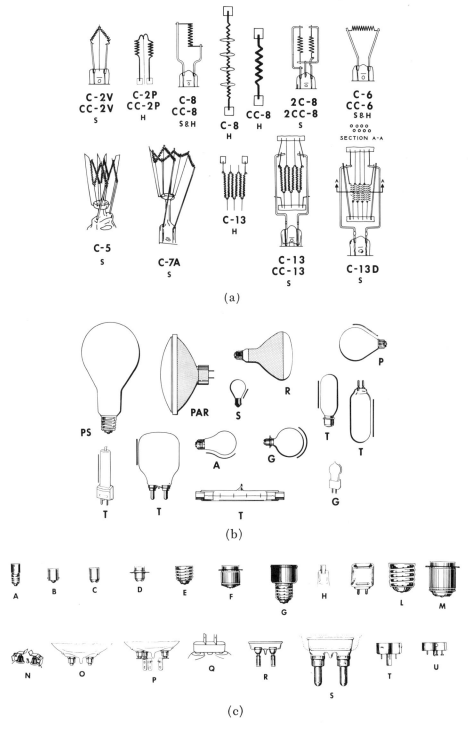

Figure 4–21 (a) Filament forms for incandescent lamps. (b) Bulb shapes for incandescent lamps. (c) Bases for incandescent lamps. (Courtesy General Electric Company, Large Lamp Department.)

have been made of other materials and bromine has been substituted for iodine for regeneration in some cases. The halogen is used to prevent blackening and improve lamp life by redepositing the evaporated tungsten on the filament. During the normal operation of an incandescent lamp, tungsten is transferred from the filament to the inside of the bulb, causing it to darken and absorb light. In the halogen lamps the iodine or bromine reacts with the evaporated tungsten, returning to the filament where it decomposes and returns the tungsten to the filament. This cycle continues throughout the life of the lamp.

The advantage of this halogen lamp is that almost 100 percent of its lumen output is maintained throughout the life of the lamp. Contrary to the limited burning position of the simple (for projection and spotlights) lamp, the halogen lamp burns in any position. The life is also much longer. While the old tungsten spotlight lamp has a usual life of 200 hours, the halogen lamp with the same filament temperature has a life of 2000 hours in some cases. In such needs as color television, higher filament temperature are desired and can be obtained in a special group of lamps with a shorter life (250 and 400 hours).

The basic tungsten halogen lamp is much more compact than common tungsten lamps. The bulb diameter is from ½ to ¾ inch (T4 and T6), and overall lengths are about 3 to 5 inches, depending on wattage (Figure 4–22).

Figure 4–22   Sylvania double-ended halogen lamps used in some ellipsoidal and Fresnel spotlights.

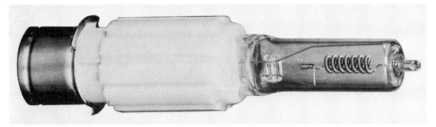

Figure 4–23 Sylvania halogen lamp for ellipsoidal spotlights, 500, 750, and 1000 watts.

As described above, many new stage lighting instruments have been designed to use these new lamps. Other manufacturers have preferred to use another form of halogen lamp in their previous models. This lamp is called "jacketed," which means that the small quartz tube is suspended in an outer bulb with a prefocus base or in some cases the medium bi-post base. These lamps then fit the standard ellipsoidal spotlights made for the base-up burning tungsten lamp such as the 500-watt T12 lamp. Larger wattage tungsten halogen lamps are on the way, and many improvements are coming along to add ruggedness, reliability, and efficiency to this important development in incandescent lighting. Two sizes and types are shown in Figures 4–23 and 4–24.

A helpful notation specifying the lamps that can be used with each spotlight can be found in some stage lighting catalogs. Both lamp catalogs and stage lighting equipment catalogs have lists of incandescent lamps, with complete data on details of sizes, shapes, and so forth, to help the user select the proper lamp for any use.

PS lamps of 1000 watts or less can be burned in any position, but G lamps cannot be burned within 45° of vertically base up. Operators must be careful in mounting spotlights to see that the lamps are burning in the proper positions, because G and T lamps will burn

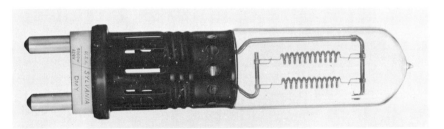

Figure 4–24 Sylvania large-wattage halogen lamp for use in lens projection and television—for base-down burning.

out quickly if placed vertically base up. PS lamps have an average life of 1000 hours, while G and T lamps for spotlight service are limited to about 200 hours. The ellipsoidal spotlight requires a tubular lamp which burns base up. It is made particularly for this instrument.

COLOR FRAMES

Frames for supporting color media used on spotlights, floodlights, and striplights are commonly made of sheet metal in two halves, with square or round openings large enough to prevent obstruction of light from the instrument for which the frame is intended. The best frames are those in which the two halves are hinged at one edge, and on the opposite edge there is riveted a fold of metal that clips the two parts together after the color medium has been inserted. Temporary frames can be cut from cardboard and held together with paper clips. One should be careful, when selecting lighting instruments, to reduce the number of color frame sizes that it is necessary to carry in stock.

MASKS AND FUNNELS (HIGH HATS)

A *mask* is a piece of sheet metal or cardboard placed within the guides of a spotlight to change the shape or size of the illuminated area. A mask may be made of a single piece with a hole cut in it, or of two pieces to allow an operator to change the size and shape of the illuminated area at will. One expensive professional mask (called an *iris*) is made like the iris diaphragm of a camera, which allows one to change the diameter of a round opening from the full size of the lens down to a pinhole or "blackout." An approximation of this can be made of two pieces of cardboard, with a triangular notch in one edge of each. Funnels, commonly called *high hats*, are frequently used to cut down on some of the "soft edge" or outer portion of the beam of a Fresnel spotlight. The larger the better, but most of these which are made as accessories for specific spotlights are not more than 12 inches long. They are made to fit the color frame guides of many spotlights. Used with ellipsoidal spotlights in anteproscenium positions, they tend to cut down spill light around the proscenium arch and on the teaser.

STAGE CABLE

A stage cable is a flexible twin conductor which consists of two bundles of fine wire, each twisted into a heavier wire like a cotton cord constructed from fine threads. Each of these conductors is covered with insulating material made of rubber or plastic. The two insulated conductors are finally covered together with more insulating material to form a single flexible cable. The safe size for use on stage in connecting spotlights, floodlights, and any other movable instrument whose total wattage is 1500 or less, is No. 14 wire, which safely carries a current of 15 amperes (see definition in Chapter 6). As 2000-watt lamps become more common, No. 12 wire is gradually replacing No. 14.

All nonprofessional workers should be warned against using cable of current-carrying capacity less than the current through the load. It is both illegal and unsafe. For example, No. 14 wire is unsafe for arc spotlights or other instruments that draw from 25 to 100 amperes. Where the wire or cable is subject to heat, asbestos-covered wire is essential. Any of the lighting equipment companies listed in the Directory of Manufacturers at the end of the book, as well as the electrical wholesalers, can supply all sorts of stage cable.

Electrical codes in many cities, and even states, require that outlets in public buildings, where extension cords are connected to electrical appliances, have a third "ground" connection, and that the cable have a third wire. In many cases this has been applied to theatres, and while the change is expensive, it is definitely in the interest of safety. A short table of wire sizes with corresponding ampere capacities for SO SJO insulation is listed here for convenience. A more complete table can be found in any handbook of wiring practice and in some catalogs of lighting equipment.

Wire Sizes Gauge Number	Maximum Ampere Capacity
18	7
16	10
14	15
12	20
10	25
8	35
6	45
4	60

STAGE CABLE CONNECTORS

The common method of connecting stage cable and lighting instruments to a source of electrical energy is by means of connectors used for the stage, called pin connectors or pin plug connectors.

They consist of small blocks of fiber with contacts on one edge and a cable entrance on the opposite edge. They belong in pairs, a line connector with a load connector. The line connector has two brass cylindrical openings that receive the brass prongs of the load connector. These connectors are used in splicing lengths of cable together, to connect the short asbestos leads from a spotlight or floodlight to a length of cable, and to make any sort of connection from portable equipment to the source of electrical energy. The line connector should always be on the "live" end (the one connected to electrical energy) of a cable, and the load connector is always placed on the short leads from the lighting instrument.

For school, college, and community theatres connectors of 15-ampere size are recommended rather than the 50-ampere stage plugs and plug receptacles ordinarily found in commercial theatres. The smaller connectors are cheaper and their exclusive use in one size throughout the theatre greatly simplifies the handling of cable, because all cable will then be interchangeable. The 15-ampere size is sufficiently large to handle all ordinary incandescent loads.

To prevent connectors from pulling apart, the cable is frequently tied before the plugs are put together. This is impossible when plugging connectors into a wall or floor pocket. At the University of Iowa a hinged, rectangular metal yoke was dropped over the connectors after they were plugged in place.

In many college and university theatres the cable and the outlets have been provided with 15- or 20-ampere Twistlock[8] connectors. The three-wire type with a ground connector is specified for nearly all new installations. By rotating the plug slightly the connectors will not disconnect accidentally.

While it is desirable to have outlets on any stage all of one size, there are occasions when an extra-large load is needed. For a 65-ampere arc lightning, a 5000-watt lamp in a lens projector or a 35-ampere lamp (2100-watt, 60-volt) for a Linnebach projector are examples. There are 50-ampere Twistlock connectors for this purpose, and a few strategically located outlets of this size will be most helpful.

CONCLUSION

This chapter has surveyed contemporary lighting instruments, effects, and accessories with brief references to the past. While an attempt has been made to include late developments, new items

---

[8] Registered mark® of the Hubbel Electric Co.

are appearing frequently. The student must keep up to date with catalogs, leaflets, and so forth if he wishes to supplement his information. The emphasis has been on the principles involved in each type of instrument to give the student fundamentals rather than the specifics that he will learn in laboratory practice. Both understanding of the principles and experience in using the equipment in production are important.

PROJECTION— PRINCIPLES AND PRACTICE

CHAPTER 5

INTRODUCTION

Projecting shadow patterns on a wall or screen for theatrical entertainment is at least as old as the early Persian puppet theatre and possibly much older, and the projection of images by means of a lens was recorded in the eighteenth century. In the nineteenth century lime light and the electric arc made bright images possible. In the early part of the twentieth century, when it became possible to construct a 1000-watt concentrated filament lamp, special moving effects were seen in dramatic production. There was little call for such effect in producing plays in the 1930's and 1940's but they still had a place in the production of opera. In recent years there

has been a revival of interest in projection, especially with lens instruments, in both commercial theatre and in community and college
dramatic production. Projectors of many types and projection screens
of varied shape are built into the scenery in countless productions.
At Indiana University Dr. Gary Gaiser has produced Wedekind's
Spring's Awakening using 10 lens projectors and several Linnebach
projectors combining both front and rear methods of projection.

LENS PROJECTORS

An older type of moving-effect lens projector, called a *sciopticon,*
appeared in the early part of this century. This instrument produces
a rather mediocre image of such things as rain, snow, clouds, blue-
birds, and rippling water in the moonlight. A large list of these and
similar hand-painted effects appeared in old catalogs for rental and
purchase (see Figure 5–1). The basic item of a sciopticon was a
spotlight with a 1000-watt lamp and a 6-inch (sometimes 8-inch)
condensing lens. To the spotlight was added a second condensing
lens whose frame held the light steel drum with guides to hold an
objective (image-producing) lens, shown in the diagram in Figure
5–2 and in the photograph in Figure 5–1. Within the drum was a
revolving disc with a transparent painted effect, illuminated by the
spotlight and projected on the screen by the objective lens. The
disc was rotated by a clock mechanism, or by an electric motor and

Figure 5–1   Sciopticon or effect
machine equipped with motor instead of clock mechanism.

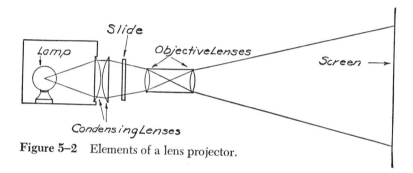

Figure 5–2   Elements of a lens projector.

reduction gears. These effects were ingenious but fairly crude. The objective lenses were inexpensive and poorly corrected. For a photographed or painted still slide, a $3\frac{1}{4}$-inch $\times$ 4-inch slide holder was substituted for the disc of the sciopticon. The San Francisco Opera Co. makes frequent use of the sciopticon and keeps at least 20 of them in stock with lenses of various focal lengths. Other opera companies, too, make use of similar equipment.

In the still version of the combination above there was nothing more than a crude lantern slide projector, somewhat like the type used for illustrated lectures. In fact, this type may be substituted if it is possible to find one with an objective of short focal length, or if space allows it to be placed far enough from the surface that receives the image.

To project a complete scenic background that will fill an ordinary drop at the rear of an average stage requires something better than the combination of parts mentioned above. It may be clearer after a brief look at the simple calculation below, but in general the whole picture can be summed up in this way. On a small or medium-size stage the acting area is likely to be quite near the scenery or cyclorama, and area light reflections and spill will wash out a projected image. Since a lens projector is an inefficient instrument (probably a little more than 5 percent of its illumination reaches the screen), the newer, better-built projectors are made for 3000- or 5000-watt lamps. The other problem, even more difficult, is the objective lens. This lens should be as large as possible, $2\frac{1}{2}$ inches to 3 inches in diameter, and the focal length must be less than 5 inches in order to produce an image 25 feet wide at a distance of about 20 feet or less. Unfortunately, many of our stages have less depth than 25 feet, and many productions might require a wider image than 20 feet. Lenses that produce rectilinear, sharp images from a 4×6 slide are very expensive. The whole instrument costs from $2000 to $3500, depending on the wattage of the lamp (3000

Figure 5–3   5000-watt Multiplate scenic projector (lens) by Thomas Wilfred, Art Institute of Light.

or 5000) and the quality and focal length of the lenses (Figure 5–3). The late Thomas Wilfred, of Clavilux fame, was one of the few people in America who promoted the use of complete background projection. Wilfred is known internationally for his development of the art of light and his beautiful and exciting effects of color and form from his Clavilux. In 1927 he applied his imagination and equipment to the production of Ibsen's *Warriors of Helgoland* at the Goodman Memorial Theatre. Those who were fortunate enough to see this projection were enthusiastic in their praise of Wilfred's projected effects, not as pure spectacle, but as an integral part of the production.

After World War II Mr. Wilfred devoted much time at his Art Institute of Light to making scene projectors for educational and civic institutions. He built projectors for a single slide and also for a remotely controlled multiple model for about 10 or 12 slides. His lamp was 5000 watts, the slide 5 inches × 6 inches, and the objective lens 5 inches in focal length. The slide and objective lens produced an image of 1 foot in width for each foot of distance to the screen. The Multiplate unit was only 12 inches thick (upstage to down) with a 45° mirror to turn the image, thus saving valuable mounting space. Ten 5-inch × 6-inch slides could be set up in advance and shifted by pushbutton remote control.[1]

While this type of equipment was expensive, some schools still

---

[1] They are no longer made.

find it a valuable money saver for scenery. Professor John Conway, supervising designer of the Theatre Department at the University of Washington, handles the scenery for several theatres and considers these scene projectors indispensable.

The television industry has stimulated a new interest in scene projection. Television studios use scene projectors frequently, having taken over and adapted many techniques from motion pictures. Both motion pictures and television have done more "rear screen" projection than projection from the front. In rear screen projection the screen is translucent and the projector is "behind" the screen, that is, on the opposite side from the actor. This makes it possible for the actor to play nearer the screen. Most stages would have insufficient depth to set up a projector 20 feet behind a screen and have any acting area remaining in front. On the other hand, if the projector is mounted above the stage on a batten or bridge, the scene can be projected over the actors' heads without much difficulty.

Figure 5–4   Kliegl 5000-watt scenic slide projector.

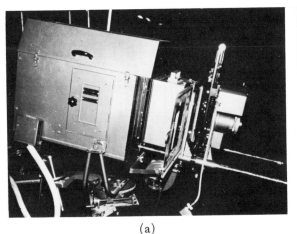

(a)

(b)

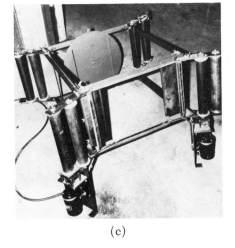

(c)

Figure 5–5 The 2500-watt xenon projector at Indiana University Theatre.

(a) Side view of the Reiche and Vogel 2500-watt xenon projector. The front assembly consists of the objective lens and a mechanical dimmer. The latter consists of two gradually darkened heat-resisting glass plates which are shifted over each other after the lamp has been dimmed as far as possible. All adjustments are calibrated to facilitate duplicating effects once a desired setting has been achieved and a record made.

(b) The Eberhard wide-angle objective lens system is able to cover a 160° expanse of cyclorama; it has two sets of slide holders and a method of tilting the entire assembly (note wingnut attachment through the slide holder opening).

(c) The motor-controlled, double-roller frame placed over and around the projector for use without any lenses. In this matter, as a direct beam projector, a wide variety of slides can be shown or continuous effects projected. The point source is 8 mm × 2 mm.

Kliegl Bros. and the Buhl Optical Co. in the United States, and Reiche and Vogel, Hugo Panni, and others in Europe, build lens projectors for the theatre (Figures 5–4 and 5–5).

In America there has been a recent wave of interest in the 35-mm lens projector for background projection in both drama and dance concerts. Some technicians are adapting a 500-watt Kodak Carousel projector to a 1000- or 1200-watt lamp with an extra blower for these short-life projection lamps. The Buhl Optical Co. makes a highly efficient adaptation of a Kodak Carousel 35-mm projector shown in

Figure 5–6 Buhl Optical Co. adaptation of Kodak Carousel lens projector.

Figure 5–6. They add the second blower for a 1200-watt quartz bromine lamp, and with their modified condensing system claim three times as much light on the screen as that produced by a 500-watt lamp. They also provide a receptacle for an electronic dissolve mechanism if one prefers this more subtle way of changing slides. Buhl is also the source of a variety of very short focus objective lenses to fit the Kodak Carousel projectors. When one is projecting a 35-mm slide over a large surface the 500-watt lamp is much too small. A 1200-watt lamp is none too large. A 1-inch focal length objective lens will produce an image of a 35-mm slide about 38 feet wide at a projection distance of 35 feet. Sample calculations are explained in the next section and tables of image size for a number of lenses manufactured by Buhl appear in their catalog.

This equipment was used effectively in a recent production of *Rosencrantz and Guildenstern Are Dead.* In this case the entire background was a projection surface shaped like an open book. Throughout the play many slides were projected from the bridge location to the screen about 20 feet distant. The remote control makes it unnecessary to have an attendant beside the projector. One note of warning might be well taken. When the images of a 35-mm slide are very large they become very grainy and do not look as well as images of smaller size. The 5000-watt projectors with slides about

4 inches × 6 inches are more satisfactory in this one respect. On the other hand, the 35-mm projector is much cheaper and the remote control quite useful.

In a recent production of Giraudoux's *Ondine* we used a lens projector for clouds in Act I. It was provided with a 5000-watt lamp and a 4-inch × 6-inch slide opening and produced a 44-foot wide image at a distance of 36 feet. The focal length of the lens was approximately 4½ inches. This projector was made by Universal Screen and had a moving attachment called a "walk along" or "crawl device." A variable-speed motor moved an 18-foot film strip of the clouds past the 4-inch × 6-inch opening at a very slow speed. The results were quite satisfactory.

Simple Calculations

The same general rule concerning lenses for spotlights applies also to lenses for projections; use a short focal length for a short throw and a long focal length for a long throw. This rule is too general, however, for the determination of image sizes, and the simple formula of relationship, familiar to every student of elementary physics, is needed.

$$\frac{1}{p} + \frac{1}{q} = \frac{1}{f}$$

p is the distance from the object (the slide) to the lens, q is the distance from the lens to the image projected on a drop or other surface, and f is the focal length of the lens.

This formula is for thin lenses, but it may be applied to thick lenses (lenses used in spotlights and projection instruments are thick) if p, q, and f are measured to the principal planes. In plano-convex lenses made of crown glass (nearly all lenses used in stage lighting are of this type), one principal plane is parallel to the plane face of the lens, within the lens, and two-thirds of the lens thickness from the plane face. The other is tangent to the convex face of the lens. Both are parallel to the plane face and perpendicular to the optical axis. p, q, and f are measured to the nearest principal plane. The sizes of the slide (S) and the image (I) are related to the p and q distances in this way.

$$\frac{S}{p} = \frac{I}{q}$$

When q is large compared with p as in the following problem, p can be considered as equal to f and the relationship becomes

$$\frac{S}{f} = \frac{I}{q}$$

S is either dimension of the slide, I is either dimension of the image, and f is the focal length.

Problem. A lens of what focal length should be used to project an image 28 feet wide with a 6-inch slide if the distance of projection is 24 feet?

$$\frac{6}{f} = \frac{28 \times 12}{24 \times 12}$$

$$F = 5.15 \text{ inches}$$

Problem. What size image can be projected from a 5-inch $\times$ 6-inch slide with a 6-inch focal length lens if the projection distance is 20 feet?

$$\frac{5}{6} = \frac{I \times 12}{20 \times 12} \qquad\qquad \frac{6}{6} = \frac{I \times 12}{20 \times 12}$$

$$I = \frac{100}{6} \qquad\qquad I = \frac{6 \times 20}{6} = 20 \text{ feet}$$

$$I = 16\tfrac{2}{3} \text{ feet}$$

The image is 20 feet by $16\tfrac{2}{3}$ feet.

The cost of a large stock of objective lenses is prohibitive for most nonprofessional organizations, but a few lenses of different focal lengths can be combined in various ways to produce a large number of focal lengths. The following relationship is used to find the focal length of the combination:

$$F = \frac{f_1 f_2}{f_1 + f_2 - s}$$

in which F is the equivalent focal length of the combination, f_1 and f_2 are the focal lengths of the two lenses, and s is the distance between them.

Problem. Given two lenses, one 8 inches and the other 12 inches in focal length, what would be the equivalent focal length if they were placed 4 inches apart?

$$F = \frac{8 \times 12}{8 + 12 - 4}$$

$F = 6$ inches, the focal length of the combination.

The problem of "distortion" has caused some difficulty in projection because it is frequently inconvenient or impossible to keep the slide parallel to the surface of the screen or cyclorama on which the image is to be projected. By distortion is meant deviation from the original design, as when parallel lines become diverging or converging, or portions of the image become large while other portions are reduced. In projecting over the heads of actors from a batten or bridge, it is necessary at times to tip the projector down

Figure 5–7   Slide with distortion made to produce normal image when projected at nonperpendicular angle from lighting bridge to cyclorama.

in order to place the image in the proper vertical position. When the projector is tipped down, a "normal slide" produces an image that is spread at the bottom and causes parallel walls of buildings to converge toward the top. To correct this distortion, the optical axis is tipped below normal and the angle is measured; the same angle is used in tipping the positive lantern slide away from parallel to the photographic enlarger. This common practice in correcting distortion produces a slide like the one in Figure 5–7. While Wilfred recommended painting the 5-inch × 6-inch slides, many American craftsmen would consider this a tedious task on so small a surface.

Many European designers, who are fond of using lens projections particularly in opera, paint their slides in place in the projector and correct the distortion (caused by projecting a flat side on a curved surface) as they paint. Our inclination in America might be to photograph the designer's sketch if the distortion problem can be

Figure 5–8   Lens projected background for Brecht's *Mother Courage*. Design by Barrett Van Loo, direction by Gordon Howard, California State University, San Diego.

handled. In Europe many theatres own eight or ten lens projectors and ingeniously paint the slides to make them "match" in a single effect composed of several images. Although lens projectors are an expensive investment for the average college theatre, they certainly can save expense and labor. In the opinion of the writer, projected scenes or parts of scenes are not appropriate for every play. The lens projector, capable of producing the fine detail, will serve a useful purpose in more realistic or naturalistic circumstances than the Linnebach (next section), but even it is not appropriate for every play. Projecting images of wallpaper or other patterns on three walls of a box set with three projectors may be interesting experimentally, but it could hardly be recommended for every contemporary realistic play.

Leaf patterns add variety, naturalistic detail, and an aesthetic touch to wall surfaces in all sorts of exterior scenes. Distortion is

Figure 5–9 Lens projected fire scene for Brecht's *Mother Courage*. Design by Barrett Van Loo, direction by Gordon Howard, lighting by H. D. Sellman, California State University, San Diego.

not a problem in this type of image. Such patterns and images appear natural because we see similar patterns of sunlight or moonlight, and shadows of various objects, around us every day. Painted sunlight and leaf shadows look decidedly unnatural unless they are part of a stylized or "period" setting. Seeing a projected scene or pattern beside a painted one is particularly distracting and inappropriate because it invites comparison between what psychologists call different "modes of appearance." A projected pattern will never look painted, and vice versa. To the writer, at least, it seems satisfactory to have a painted foreground or wall of a set, and a projected pattern of distant objects on the cyclorama. This is not distracting, perhaps because distant objects always have a hazier outline than do objects in the foreground. Projected effects actually give the appearance of being farther away.

In a recent professional opera production there were solid, conventionally painted scenic forms right and left in several scenes, with a fairly wide expanse of blue-gray cyclorama between. In one

Figure 5–10   Lens projected background for Purcell's *Dido and Aeneas*. At the University Playhouse at the University of Washington, stage design by John Ashby Conway, photography by Dorothy Conway, Seattle.

scene there was a projected pattern on this cyclorama that seemed unattached to either side and was, to the writer, completely incomprehensible. In another scene this space was filled with a hand-painted pattern of a serpent-like Nile, with suggestions of pyramids along its banks. This might have been acceptable but for two massive stone columns that must, because of their size, have belonged to the foreground. In places, however, the sketchy lines of the pyramid forms crossed over the huge columns. In a final scene this same space was filled with a photographed rectangular rope pattern that seemed to suggest prison bars through which could be seen fragments of architectural ruins. Not only did the designer attempt to project patterns of light onto painted forms to suggest the walls of a room, but he tried to suggest distant land-

Figure 5–11   Lens projection by John Ashby Conway, University Playhouse, University of Washington, for the opera, *The Barber of Seville.* Photography by Dorothy Conway, Seattle.

scape at the same time. Furthermore, he mixed styles by painting some slides and employing photographs for others. Some interesting sets that make good use of lens projected effects appear in Figures 5–8 through 5–11.

LINNEBACH PROJECTORS

While the more expensive lens projector is better for a sharp image and the projection of fine detail, the Linnebach, or shadowgraph, projector is better for broad, wide-angle effects in which detail is unimportant. The lens projector is limited in spread to very little more width of image than the projection distance, perhaps a 26-foot width for a projection distance of 20 feet. On the other hand, the Linnebach will cover a whole cyclorama through an angle of 180° if desired. The lens projector works well when projecting images on a plane or almost plane surface, but the Linnebach can project a slightly fuzzy image on a cyclorama of any shape, as well as on a plane surface (drop). Lamps of lower wattage (500 to 2000 watts) are also satisfactory in Linnebach projectors. The best I have found is 2100 watts, 60 volts.

On the realistic side, city skylines, distant hills and mountains and clouds are about all one can expect from Linnebach projectors because they are really at their best in expressionism, stylized images, and fantasy.

The Linnebach projector is so simple that any craftsman in the nonprofessional theatre can construct one, at least with the help of a sheet-metal shop. Basically, it is a socket and lamp inside a black box with guides for the slide. Theoretically, one needs a point source of light which will produce a sharp image or shadow of the opaque and transparent elements in the slide. Since the smallest filament in a lamp producing enough light is probably ½ inch wide by ⅝ inch high, the image inevitably will have a fuzzy outline. Anyone who has stood between a light source and a wall knows that the closer one is to the source, the larger the image or shadow, and the fuzzier the outline of the shadow. Each part of the filament tends to make a separate shadow of the slide. A general rule, accordingly, is to use the smallest filament possible and to have the slide as far as possible from the filament. A number of practical considerations, however, must enter here. Unless the stage is quite small, a 1000-watt lamp is needed. Projection lamps have the smallest filaments, but their life is short. Keeping the slide as far as possible from the lamp has its limits because the Linnebach hood

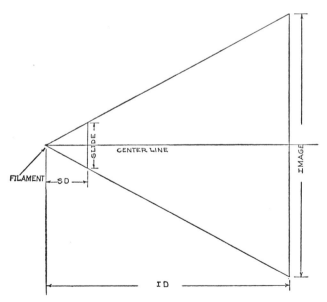

Figure 5–12   Linnebach diagram.

will become unwieldy and the material for the slide is hard to find in pieces larger than 20 inches × 50 inches.

The calculations of slide and image size are quite simple, since they deal with the simple proportion in the corresponding parts of similar triangles. It is well to lay out the whole problem graphically to scale on the ground plan and longitudinal section through the stage. Referring now to the diagram in Figure 5–12, it should be clear that the apex of both triangles is at the filament of the lamp in the Linnebach hood. The base of the small triangle is the slide S and its altitude is the slide distance (filament to slide) SD. The base of the large triangle is the image on a cyclorama or drop (screen) and its altitude is the image distance (ID) measured from the filament to the image on the drop or cyclorama.

$$\frac{S}{I} = \frac{\text{slide distance (SD)}}{\text{image distance (ID)}}$$

Problem. In a Linnebach projector the lamp filament is 2 feet from the slide, and the projection distance (filament to drop) is 18 feet. If the slide is 20 inches high and 36 inches wide, what will the size of the image be?

$$\frac{20}{I} = \frac{2 \times 12}{18 \times 12} \qquad\qquad \frac{36}{I} = \frac{2 \times 12}{18 \times 12}$$

$$I = 15 \text{ feet} \qquad\qquad\qquad I = 27 \text{ feet}$$

The image will be 15 feet by 27 feet.

When a plane slide is used to project an image on a flat drop, there is no distortion of the image if the slide and drop are parallel. This is not difficult if the projector is mounted on a batten or bridge and the image is projected over the actors' heads. The projectors are sometimes placed behind scenery, such as a ground row, since a very wide angle is possible with this instrument. Again, the slide and image can be kept parallel. If it is possible to keep the slide vertical like the drop, the resulting distortion can be corrected by laying the image out on paper in plotted squares and working back to the slide.

On stages large enough for a sky cyclorama, the Linnebach projector is ideal for covering this surface with any sort of appropriate image (keeping in mind the Linnebach's limitations mentioned above) all the way around to the downstage extremities, up to 180°. If the cyclorama is a semicylinder, the hood shape and slide must be the same to avoid distortion problems. In fact, if the cyclorama is a deviation from a true semicylinder, with a flatter area in center rear and a slightly shorter radius where it turns downstage, it makes no difference. One simply shapes the hood and slide of the projector to duplicate that of the surface on which the image is projected. No distortion results if the projector is centered with respect to the image, and the slide and image are parallel.

Sometimes it is desirable to have more than one Linnebach projector mounted along a batten or lighting bridge, so that the hood is not centered. For example, a different image may be needed for each of several scenes, with no time for changing the slides between scenes. Or perhaps the play calls for a transformation, such as that in *Blue Bird* when the graveyard turns into a fairy garden. If the two Linnebachs are side by side, one is dimmed down as the other is dimmed up. There are many such transformations in fantasy and expressionism. In Kaiser's *From Morn 'til Midnight* the tree changes into a skeleton as the bank clerk watches it. Again, it is a matter of two projections, one dimming out as the other is dimmed up. To prevent distortion, when the projector is moved from the center, the lamp should be moved a proportional distance in the same direction in the Linnebach hood. It is simple enough if an adjustment for moving the socket is provided when the Linnebach is built.

Linnebach slides are easier to paint and construct than lens projector slides, since they are so much larger. A very simple slide can be cut from cardboard, with a distant mountain as a horizon outline, and open sky produced by a single light-blue sheet of color medium. Plastic sheets, heavy enough to prevent buckling, can be used as Linnebach slides without being framed. Colored plastic or gelatin shapes can be glued to the surface to form a design; special transparent lacquers or water paints, such as KOH-I-NOOR transparent acetate ink, made to adhere to plastic sheets, are available to those who wish to paint the design. One must be careful about solvent for thinning or correcting mistakes; some solvents tend to dissolve the plastic sheets and make the slide translucent. This will diffuse the light and spoil the image. Slides must be transparent.

Some years ago a magazine article[2] about the work of Boris Aronson suggested an imaginative use of projected images. Although Aronson worked with a model and a lens projector, the idea could be applied to Linnebach projection even more effectively. Not only did he make helpful suggestions concerning the preparation of slides, but he suggested breaking the surface of the image screen (cyclorama or drop) by applying different kinds of materials to the surface, such as opaque, open-mesh screen, and fabric to break up and change the image in a variety of ways.

[2] *The Magic Lantern*, "Interiors" (Dec. 1948).

Figure 5–13 2100-watt, 60-volt lamp direct beam scenic projector with sky drum by Thomas Wilfred, Art Institute of Light (no longer built).

Figure 5–14 Linnebach clouds projected by single plane slide to back wall of stage for a scene from *West Side Story*. Design by Don W. Powell, California State University, San Diego.

Thomas Wilfred had a Direct Beam Projector (his name for his version of the Linnebach projector) that was more completely described along with lens projectors in his monograph[3] on this subject. This was a Linnebach-type projector with several unique features. The light source was a 2100-watt, 60-volt lamp with a 6-volt control circuit blower and heat absorbing filter. While its maximum spread was 90°, its "color modifier" was an asset that put this projector out of the home-made class. Strips of progressively graded colors were mounted in two motor-driven frames which could be moved in opposite directions at very slow speeds. He suggested lighting the cyclorama with this projector even without slides, since his "color modifier" would change sky from daylight, through sunset, to night. A motor-driven plastic drum (on which one could paint clouds or other objects) moved around the instrument to add to his sky effects. Mr. Wilfred suggested that "landscape" slides be set up in front of the projector with the distant portion of the scene nearer the projector, and the foreground on a larger slide set farther away so that this portion of the image would be sharper. He suggested painting the slides on glass when projecting on a drop. The Thomas Wilfred Direct Beam Projector is shown in Figure 5–13.

While neither lens projections nor Linnebach projections have a place in every production, they are useful elements of scenery and lighting. Although no substitutes for canvas and wood, projected scenes or images make many productions more convincing and dramatically effective.

---

[3] Thomas Wilfred, *Projected Scenery, A Technical Manual* (West Nyack, N.Y., Art Institute of Light, 1955).

COLOR

CHAPTER 6

INTRODUCTION

"Light is the aspect of radiant energy of which a human observer is aware through the visual sensations which arise from stimulation of the retina."[1] Light, defined in this way, is a psychophysical concept. It is safe to say that, in their broadest sense, color and light are practically synonymous. If radiant energy from the sun passes through water vapor and stimulates the retina of the eye of the

[1] *1944 Report of the Colorimetry Committee of the Optical Society of America.* In this chapter an attempt will be made to follow this report as far as definitions are concerned.

96

observer, it is seen as a rainbow. When similar radiant energy is made to pass through a triangular prism of glass, we call the observed result, as it stimulates the retina, a spectrum or band of color composed of violet, blue, green, yellow, orange, and red. These colors have wavelengths from 400 millimicrons to 700 millimicrons, and thus form the visible spectrum.

According to the strict interpretation of our definition, it is not accurate to attribute colors to objects but only to the light reflected from them. Radiant energy falls on an object, and its color is nothing more than its ability to modify the light incident upon it. The object absorbs certain wavelengths; others reach the retina of the observer. The color of an object, then, depends on (1) the spectral distribution of incident radiant energy, (2) selective absorption, (3) and the psychophysical functions of human vision.

When light falls on the surface of an object, one of three things can happen: the light may be absorbed, reflected, or transmitted. When radiant energy falls on an object that is ordinarily called red (the way it appears in daylight), other wavelengths are absorbed, and red wavelengths (if any are present) are reflected to the eye of the observer, who perceives the object as red. This is selective reflection. If the red material is transparent, less energy may be reflected from the surface, but essentially the material transmits red and absorbs the other wavelengths.

The Colorimetry Committee of the Optical Society of America used the term *luminance* in referring to the effect on the eye of light direct from its source, and *reflectance* when the light comes from a surface that has reflected the light. *Brightness* is the technical term they have adopted when referring to the mental effect of light of a specific luminance. As brightness refers to luminance, so *lightness* refers to reflectance. Luminance and reflectance are psychophysical terms. Brightness and lightness are psychological terms.

Brightness (or lightness), then, is the attribute of a color which makes it equivalent to one member of an achromatic series, ranging from very dim to very bright (brightness), and from black to white.

There are innumerable color systems, some with color solids in which there is a vertical axis that forms a gray scale, with white at the top and black at the bottom. In the Munsell System[2] the three variables are hue, chroma, and value, which correspond roughly to hue, saturation, and brightness (or lightness) of the Optical Society's Colorimetry Report. Munsell called his gray series a scale of value instead of a scale of lightness.

[2] A. H. Munsell, *A Color Notation* (Baltimore, Munsell Color Co., Inc., 1946).

A German system of color, invented by Wilhelm Ostwald,[3] uses a double cone as a color solid with a gray scale through the center, white at the upper apex, and black at the lower. His gray scale corresponds to a series of illumination intensities which would make it behave according to psychophysical variable rather than psychological ones. These two systems help us to understand surface colors and their variables.

Returning to the definitions of the other two attributes of color, they are as follows: *Hue* is that attribute of color which permits it to be classified as red, orange, yellow, green, blue-green, blue, violet, and so forth. Chromatic colors are those possessing hue. Achromatic colors are those which have no hue; that is, they correspond to the gray scale mentioned above, and range from very dim to very bright. *Saturation* is that attribute of any chromatic color which determines its degree of difference from the achromatic color that it resembles most closely. These three, *brightness* (or *lightness*), *hue*, and *saturation*, are the most common terms for the attributes of color sensation.

ADDITIVE AND SUBTRACTIVE MIXTURES

As was mentioned above, when light strikes an object it is reflected, absorbed, or transmitted. If the object is transparent, a small amount of light is reflected, and certain wavelengths are absorbed while others are transmitted. This is considered a subtractive mixture. When white light falls on a transparent red color medium, a small amount of white light is reflected from the surface, the exact quantity depending on the angle at which the light strikes the surface. Red is transmitted, and the remainder of the white light is absorbed (subtracted). If a transparent green filter were placed in the path of the red light, the red would be absorbed by the green filter and nothing would be transmitted.

When two different lights (with different wavelength distributions), such as a red and a green, fall on the same surface and are reflected to the eye, they reach the eye as a single distribution, in this case yellow. Green is added to red and reaches the eye as yellow. This is called an additive mixture. All of the changes in light before it reaches the eye work according to the additive or subtractive process.

[3] Wilhelm Ostwald, *Color Science* (London, Winston & Newton, Ltd., 1931, 1933).

ADDITIVE PRIMARIES

White light (sunlight) is a mixture of the visible wavelengths from 400 to 700 millimicrons. When light passes through a prism to form a band of color, the separate colors are usually recognized as violet, blue, green, yellow, orange, and red. Sir. Isaac Newton was the first to observe this, and later it was discovered that if three widely separated colors are projected to a white surface it is possible to match the appearance of any other part of the spectrum. All three of these together will produce white light. There are also a large number of pairs of colors which, when mixed, will produce white—for example, blue and yellow (complementary colors).

For an accurate mathematical specification, it would be well to follow the approach accepted by the Optical Society of America, the I.C.I. (International Commission on Illumination) system. This system involves the specification of a color in terms of the amounts of three I.C.I. standard primaries (standard lights). A complete description of this system is beyond the scope and elementary nature of this chapter, but can be found in a number of books on color systems.[4]

For practical use in the theatre it is possible to use three saturated glass or plastic (transparent) color filters, blue, green, and red, for the additive primaries. The principles involved in understanding the additive primaries can be illustrated best by reference to an equilateral triangle shown in Figure 6–1. Here, light is being mixed from two or three separate light sources, each with a primary color medium covering the incandescent lamp. In stage lighting terms, three color filters are each being placed in front of the lens of a spotlight, and are projecting their beams to a single area. Blue and green in various proportions will obviously produce all of the possibilities from a slightly bluish green to a slightly greenish blue. If we accept the name *magenta* for the half-and-half mixture of blue and red, then various proportions of red and blue might be purple, through magenta, to a scarlet red. Green and red additive mixtures are a little more surprising to those who are meeting this phase of color for the first time. Approximately equal parts of green and red produce yellow. With more green than red, yellow-green is produced; and with more red than green, the result will be orange. Mixtures are inclined to be brighter and less saturated than the basic primaries. When two colors such as blue-green and red (or green and magenta, or blue and yellow) are projected to a white surface,

---

[4] Ralph M. Evans, *An Introduction to Color* (New York, John Wiley & Sons, Inc., 1948), and in numerous technical periodicals.

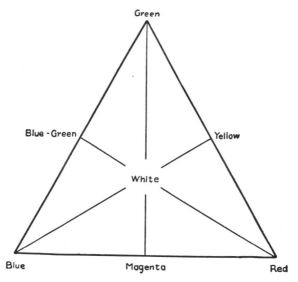

Figure 6–1   Additive mixture of color.

the result will be white light. Such pairs producing white are called complementary colors, or complements. When all three of the primaries are mixed from three different light sources, a large number of other colors can be produced by varying the proportions of the three. After two colors are mixed and a third one is added, the resultant mixture and the third color become diluted until the result is white light. This is common practice when the striplights are wired in three circuits and the lamps are covered with primary blue, green, and red color media. Projected to a light-blue cyclorama, an approximately equal mixture of the three reveals the cyclorama as a daylight sky. By adjusting the dimmer readings on these three color circuits one can produce the various tints and colors of a sunset, after which he can gradually dim out the red and green to the desired dark blue (or combination of dim blue and a small amount of green) for a color that resembles a night sky on this same cyclorama. Although primary colors are rarely used in spotlights for acting area lighting, light tints of blue, blue-green, yellow, violet, and red are common and are used in spotlights where two are focused on one area. This is an example of additive mixtures in specific illumination. It is possible under special circumstances to use more saturated colors in acting area spotlights. If, in a stylized production, one wishes to exaggerate the color in shade or shadows, he can use complementary saturated colors in spotlights, depending on the additive mixture to produce white highlights, and a white undistorting mixture on the make-up, while the saturated color falls in the folds of the costumes, one color on one side, the other on the opposite side.

SUBTRACTIVE MIXTURES

As mentioned above, when light is transmitted or absorbed selectively, some wavelengths are subtracted, so less light reaches the eye than the original amount emanating from the source. This is a subtractive process. Our general understanding of primary colors is that a few fundamental colors are capable of being combined to produce a great many others. The three that seem to produce the greatest number of nearly saturated colors are called cyan (or blue-green), yellow, and magenta. Referring to the superimposed circles in Figure 6–2, one can see that blue over magenta produces blue, magenta over yellow produces red, and blue-green over yellow produces green. Superimposing all three produces gray or black. One should think of this subtractive mixing as the placement of one transparent color medium, such as a colored gelatin filter, over another. In fact, this is actually done in stage lighting practice when one fails to find in stock the exact tint he needs. If a daylight blue filter seems to be too green (blue-green) for a particular costume or make-up color, a lavender (pale magenta) filter can be placed over it to produce a color that is nearer pure blue. Perhaps a yellow medium is too greenish (lemon yellow) for a pleasant sunlight color; a lavender or pink filter will subtract the green wavelengths and produce a more desirable straight yellow.

Dyes are transparent colors that mix subtractively, as do transparent water-color paints. While painters rarely limit themselves to three pigments, Dr. Herbert Ives[5] made a quantitive spectral analysis of many pigment colors and found that fairly good results could be obtained with the three primaries—blue-green, magenta, and yellow.[6] He concluded that there were certain deficiencies in available pigments and that at least four colors might be better than three.

Theoretically, a subtractive primary would have to transmit more than a narrow band of spectral energy in order to fulfill the requirement that two colors superimposed produce a third color. For example, both blue-green and magenta will transmit blue because

[5] Herbert Ives, "Thomas Young and the Simplification of the Artist's Palette," *Proceedings of the Physical Society* (Jan. 1934).

[6] The water colors suggested were prussian blue (pure ferric ferrocyanide), rhodamine 6G lake, and cadmium yellow.

they have blue in them, but blue and red have nothing in common to transmit; so theoretically they will transmit nothing when superimposed. In practice, however, there are few, if any, color filters that are so selective. Nearly all blue filters transmit a small amount of green or blue-green.

PIGMENT MIXTURES

As mentioned in the last section, transparent water colors mix according to subtractive principles. There are, however, many pigments that are not transparent. Opaque pigment particles may cover each other and only the top layer will reflect certain wavelengths to the eye. Particles that reflect different wavelengths when placed side by side will produce results according to the additive mixture principle. If a surface is painted with small dots of two different colors and viewed at a distance, the eye does not see the separate dots. If the dots are blue and yellow, this surface will appear gray when seen at a distance in a white light. This is an additive mixture because the blue and yellow reflected from the dots mix before they reach the eye. While we might call this mixture white light, the lightness level of such a surface would not be high enough to call the surface white. It might be a medium gray, depending on the average lightness of the blue and yellow. Since the behavior of pigment mixtures may be either additive or subtractive, it is difficult to predict the results of mixtures except by experience with specific pigments. The spatter method of scene painting is essentially an additive mixture, unless the pigments are transparent and some of the dots cover others, in which case light can pass through transparent dots and this part of the result is subtractive.

THE LIGHT SOURCE

The use of the common incandescent lamp, modified by selective transmission and absorption in the form of color filters, is our basic method of revealing and changing the appearance of objects and people on the stage. Although the incandescent lamp is not entirely satisfactory in spectral distribution, it is a fairly small source that can be dimmed satisfactorily. The spectral distribution leaves much to be desired, since it is quite low on the violet and blue end, and high on the orange and red. The mixture of wavelengths is a pale yellowish white that changes gradually into red as the lamp is dimmed until almost no blue energy is produced. Sources with more

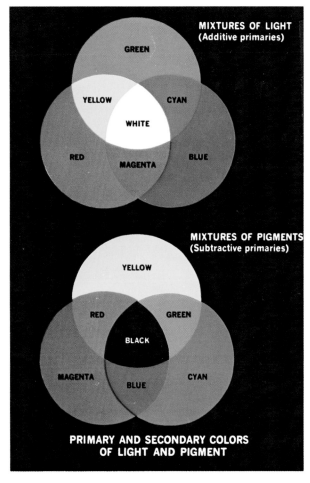

Figure 6–2 Additive mixture above, subtractive mixture below. (Courtesy General Electric Company.)

blue, such as fluorescent lamps, are more efficient but are more difficult to dim and cannot be used in spotlights. They are used in open-pan floodlights for television to a limited extent, but are not gaining in popularity. Carbon arcs produce a white light with a smaller source but cannot be dimmed. Zenon, mercury vapor, and mercury iodide are all whiter but cannot be dimmed satisfactorily. See Chapter 4.

COLOR MEDIA

Color filters currently accessible are far from satisfactory. The following sections will show simple comparisons of such qualities as range of color, durability, fading, and cost. Better materials at lower cost would be made in this country if there were greater demand.

Transparent Lacquer

Transparent lacquer that can be applied directly to the bulb of an incandescent lamp is available in five or six colors, and these can be mixed to produce others. It fades easily and is burned off rapidly in lamps larger than 50 watts. It is useful in coloring a few lamps for backing striplights and for painting slides for projection.

Glass

Colored glass roundels that fit over individual lamps or reflectors in borderlights, footlights, and striplight sections have been common for many years. They are made of heat-resistant glass in different sizes and shapes, but are limited to a few colors like red, green, blue, yellow, and clear. The so-called primary colors are quite satisfactory for mixing the other colors needed for the cyclorama, including sunsets, and for toning and blending the acting area with general illumination. Although the roundels are expensive, their colors do not fade. Various tints in glass strips, framed in the usual color frame sizes for spotlights, have been available for several years. These are expensive and heavy, but with good care will last a long time. Since they are handled much more than roundels in striplights, breakage is much higher.

Gelatin

Colored sheets of gelatin are still the most popular for use in spotlights and have survived a number of newer materials. Gelatin is available in about 100 hues and tints in sheets approximately 20 inches × 24 inches. The cost is around 35 cents a sheet. Its only advantages are its low cost, large variety of colors, and flameproof quality. It fades easily, is easily dehydrated in dry climates or in heated storage places. When dry, it is brittle and fragile, its usual condition after a short time in a hot spotlight. All the colors seem to fade, especially the blues and blue-greens, which last no more than 6 or 8 hours when in use.

Plastic Color Media

Cinemoid is an imported plastic medium made in England. It is made in a large number of colors and tints that have been useful for a number of years. The plastic material is thicker and stiffer than gelatin but still not thick enough to use without color frames. The price is about $1.30 for a sheet about 20 inches × 24 inches. This material is flameproof and mechanically strong, but fades about as fast as gelatin. A new material called Dynamoid made by the Celanese Corp. has recently appeared. It is a laminated plastic, possibly a little thinner than the other, but is available in about the same colors at a slightly lower price. Several gelatin dealers are now offering plastics. Since the fading is about the same, it is difficult to decide whether the plastic or the gelatin is more economical to use. It is probably a toss up.

COLOR SELECTION

Color selection is certainly a matter of personal preference as well as good common sense, but it seems to the author that a large number of hues and tints in color media is unnecessary. Many of the available colors are so close together in hue that it is almost impossible to tell the difference when used on a cyclorama or on the acting area, especially on the acting area mixed additively with another color. At one time a color medium called "chocolate" was highly desirable as an acting area color. I see nothing in it but an unsaturated pink or orange pink that is very low in light transmission. Pink is a useful acting area color but, of course, one needs a bluish pink at one time and an orange pink at another to meet the needs of make-up and costume, as well as mood and atmosphere. As mentioned elsewhere, highly saturated colors distort make-up and costume too much and are rarely used for the acting area. "Surprise pink," a lavender that emphasizes both ends of the spectrum but cuts down the middle portion, the yellow, is probably the most useful and flattering of all the possibilities in lighting the acting area. Here, too, there are variations to suit individual taste and desires for the particular occasion, and since incandescent light is yellowish, lavenders are helpful in giving the actor a less sallow, more vital appearance.

To give a cool appearance to the scene nothing serves as well as a light tint of blue, ordinarily referred to as daylight blue. This color medium tends to remove more red than the lavender tints. When used alone the effect can be quite cold, especially if the color tends toward medium blue. Medium blue used alone is ordinarily too saturated and causes distortions in costume and make-up. One must be careful in the selection of light blues for make-up because a greenish appearance for the actor may make him look ill or unpleasant. As mentioned elsewhere, one must compensate in making up for a stage lighted with much blue light. Yellow or amber is the other basic color frequently used to light the acting area. A greenish yellow is undesirable almost anywhere, but a pleasant amber or pinkish amber is excellent for sunlight on the stage and looks well on the actor as he walks in and out of it to be relieved in appearance by other tints. Amber or yellow from both directions over the whole area gives the actor a sallow appearance, not always desirable for every age and condition. Mr. Howard Bay, the New York designer, used blue from one direction and amber from the other in his recent production of *Man of la Mancha.* Since blue and yellow produce white additively, the yellow or amber was not overpowering, especially when he used some white "fill" light from the balcony front.

These four—amber, daylight blue, pink, and lavender—form a good basic palette for acting area lighting. When they are elaborated by cool and warm variants of each and some variation in saturation, a high degree of variety and subtlety are possible to accomplish the function of lighting the acting area.

For lighting the cyclorama or a sky drop a primary blue is suitable for most instances of a night sky, but the color of the cyclorama material must be considered as well as the other purposes besides realism for which the cyclorama might serve. For a daylight sky there are several light blue tints such as daylight blue, light blue, steel blue, and others, depending on the color of cyclorama, the play itself, and the personal preferences of the scene designer and lighting director. The three primary colors—blue, green and red—furnished by striplight sections—do fairly well for the variations of a day and night sky, sunrise and sunset, and even many unusual effects when the striplights light the lower part of the cyclorama from the stage floor.

FLUORESCENCE AND PHOSPHORESCENCE

There are a large number of substances such as minerals and dyes that are stimulated to "glow" or become luminous when certain wavelengths fall upon them. These wavelengths are invisible and shorter than 4000 angstroms in the spectrum. These invisible wavelengths are changed into visible light by fluorescent materials.

Phosphorescent materials are different in that they seem to store the invisible energy from ultraviolet wavelengths and continue to phosphoresce or "glow" after the ultraviolet source has been removed. Both materials are available in paint and in stage make-up. Phosphorescent and fluorescent effects are not very common in the production of plays, but these so-called "black light" effects are common in musicals, reviews, and night club acts. The "black light" or ultraviolet source is available for rental or purchase as a unit consisting of a ballast and reflector with a mogul socket for a mercury vapor lamp at 250 watts and an ultraviolet glass color medium. The ultraviolet energy is quite low, and several of these units are needed for an average-size stage. My experience has indicated that four to six ultraviolet 40-watt, 48-inch fluorescent lamps in common fluorescent luminares produce more energy at less expense than two of the standard "black light" instruments. This standard instrument requires 5 minutes to warm up, and the 40-watt fluorescent lamps start instantly.

LIGHT AND COSTUME

Although it is rarely done, the color of the light in which the costume will be worn by all means should be considered when the costume is designed. Using colored light in the dye room, or looking at the material through small pieces of color media will help a great deal to prevent redyeing after the first dress rehearsal. In general, unsaturated colors in light are much safer than saturated ones for period costumes that are made of several colors, but even with such acting area colors as daylight blue and amber, light-colored costumes can be considerably affected. For example, a yellow costume can be grayed or neutralized by daylight blue light, and it will be black in saturated blue light. The reverse is also true. A blue costume is grayed by light amber illumination, and yellow-orange light will make the blue look absolutely black. Generalizing, one can say that light of a complementary hue will make a costume appear gray, but light of a similar hue will enhance the beauty of a piece of fabric and make it more prominent. Blue light on blue velvet or satin makes it seem to glow from within. In dimly illuminated scenes costumes should be of tints if possible, because they need to reflect more light than the background, while in well-lighted scenes saturated hues and shades may also be included. The designer of costumes, all will agree, should have a thorough understanding of color in light as well as color in fabrics.

LIGHT AND MAKE-UP

One who is responsible for the lighting of a play is often held responsible for deficiencies in make-up, but make-up is really the actor's problem, and he should include in his training some consideration of the way light affects his appearance. In general, foundation make-up has more red in it than normal flesh color, because much amber light has been common in stage lighting. Heavy foundations now are out of style, because more suitable colors in light, like daylight blue, very light amber, and pink, are in more general stage use. Illusion pink (a highly unsaturated violet) is a flattering color medium that passes all of the spectrum but is low in yellow. For this reason, it takes away sallowness and emphasizes the pink pigment in the actor's complexion.

The following simple suggestions about make-up and colored light may prove useful.

Amber light adds a yellow tonality that tends to make the complexion sallow, and reduces the contrast between rouge and foundation. More rouge, or rouge with less orange in it, is necessary.

Red light is reflected by rouge and foundation equally, leaving the actor apparently with no rouge. More rouge slightly toward the blue is necessary in red light.

Blue light has the opposite effect. Red reflects little or no blue light; therefore in blue light, rouge on the cheeks appears as two black spots. A very light foundation, with only a trace of rouge, is best in blue light.

Green light gives the face an unearthly appearance and should be avoided unless the play demands such an effect.

Professional actors and some experienced nonprofessionals are very familiar with these suggestions, but a surprising number of players lack even a trace of information of this sort.

LIGHT AND SCENERY

The radical lighting designer is of the opinion that scenery is merely one of the reflectors that he needs in making a design in light. While most scenic artists would probably disagree, this is, from a technical view at least, essentially true, and in this way it will be considered for the moment. Ideally, acting area light should be kept off the scenery, but reflections from the floor and spill light influence its appearance to some degree. As in the case of costumes, scenery must be designed and painted for a specific color in lighting. Otherwise it will never look as it was intended. Scenery, as most people in the theatre know, should almost never be painted in a flat color, but by one technique or another several colors should be applied, so that definite spots or small areas of each color lie near each other. When light falls on the whole surface, each small area reflects certain parts of the spectrum, and the reflected light mixes additively before it reaches the eye some distance away in the auditorium. If the primaries, blue, green, and red, were painted on the surface in this way and illuminated with white light, the surface at a distance would appear gray, but very different from one with a uniform gray paint covering the whole surface. The one with the three colors would have texture, variety, and beauty, while the solid color surface would be monotonous. If the three colors were illuminated with red light, the blue and green would reflect no light, and the appearance at a distance would be that of a dark red, uneven surface, uneven because of the areas reflecting no light. By changing the light to blue, the color of the surface would appear as dark blue. Changes in the color of light frequently assist in scene changes, but the painting must be done with this definite intention. It is not, however, so simple as it sounds. The primaries are rarely, if ever, used, but several colors more appropriate to the particular design are used, along with a color in the general illumination that will emphasize the dominant color in the paint. Three-circuit striplights, with blue, green, and red filters, mounted on the bridge or first pipe along with the acting area spotlights, can serve the purpose of toning and blending the walls of an interior set. The footlights, although rarely used, can also assist in this way. As the mood changes from act to act in a single-set production, this mood can be suggested by progressing from a warm to a cool tonality (or vice versa) by varying the mixture of the three colors in the general illumination. The set, of course, must be painted to reflect this change.

Monk's cloth, hemp, and other neutral (gray) materials used as draperies for the stage are easily colored by means of striplights and floodlights with appropriate color media. Because of their sheen and the interesting highlights and shade when they are hung in folds, silk, satin, and rayon look well in colored light. All of these materials should be hung in folds in order to attain variety in light and shade. If light from opposite directions is of different colors, one can have shadows of two different colors and an additive mixture of these colors in the highlights.

By carefully selecting pigments that have a distinctly different appearance in two or more colors in light, spectacular and comic effects are possible for the right occasion (not usually for drama). As an illustration, one can draw two sketches on white paper, one with blue chalk and one with orange or red chalk. In blue light the blue chalk and the white paper are equally blue because each reflects blue light to about the same degree; so the blue sketch essentially disappears. The orange chalk, reflecting little or no blue light, appears black and stands out boldly. In red light the orange or red chalk disappears and the blue sketch appears. Very amusing cartoons can be made in this way and changed by changing the color of the light. One might paint a drop according to these principles and change a woodland scene from summer to winter. If the sky were light blue and the leaves of the trees green or blue-green, the leaves could be made to disappear by using green or blue-green light. Such things have to be very well done to have any measure of success, and such a drop could not be shown in its entirety. If only a part of it were seen through windows, it might be satisfactory. In general though, such things are too spectacular for drama, and belong to musical comedy and revues, where smart effects are always in demand.

Good designers should know the relationship of light to pigment so thoroughly that they think in terms of light even when using pigments. Sorrowful is he who paints a set for amber light and discovers later that his set will be "clothed" in daylight blue.

COLOR SYMBOLISM

The use of light for emotional and psychological purposes was discussed briefly in Chapter 1. Although this function is somewhat intangible, its usefulness and definite place in lighting on the stage are established. Research in this field is needed but is difficult to approach. The related subject of color symbolism is fraught with many contradictions, and its use with many pitfalls. For certain plays, nevertheless, there is a definite place for symbolism in costumes and lighting. In such cases, if it is used with clarity and simplicity, it should be successful. True, there is considerable divergence of opinion, and colors certainly do affect people in a great variety of ways.

For these reasons it has been considered of sufficient importance to mention some of the ideas and to present a list of the things which colors are said to symbolize and suggest. In some cases there is substantial agreement. Red, orange, and yellow are commonly called warm hues, and blue and green are said to be cool. A certain hue of red may suggest murder because blood is associated with murder. It also suggests anger, perhaps because a bull is supposed to be angered by red. Green is generally agreed upon as suggesting envy under certain conditions.

Color on the stage is used primarily, of course, for other reasons, but it has been discovered, sometimes by accident, that color affects an audience emotionally—at times objectionably so. The atmosphere of a scene or complete play often suggests certain hues to an artist. To be sure, the same play probably suggests entirely different hues to another artist, and it is difficult to say who is right. For example, red, orange, and yellow light might be used for the drinking scenes in *Twelfth Night* and *Henry IV*. Purple and red would suggest royalty and power in throne-room scenes. The projection of dagger-like shafts of red light for a murder scene in *Macbeth* is obviously symbolic.

This brings us to a clue to the mystery of the many conflicting ideas associated with various hues. Color can be used with so many other things that influence the impression it makes on an audience that one can never state arbitrarily what a hue symbolizes unless the circumstances are included. For example, form alone can change the emotional or symbolic value of a hue entirely. A dagger pattern of red light surrounding Macbeth when he says, "Is this a dagger, which I see before me, the handle toward my hand?" could hardly suggest anything but Macbeth's state of mind as he plans to murder Duncan. On the other hand, a red costume for a king might well indicate royalty and power. To use color effectively for this purpose, one must always consider form, associated hues, and all of the surrounding elements that influence the emotional and symbolic value of a color.

A glance at the following list will show what a diversity of ideas is associated with a single hue. These have been taken from countless literary sources of all ages, and are included here as a possible aid in designing costumes, scenery, and lighting.

White is the symbol of light, purity, chastity, innocence, truth, modesty, peace, femininity, delicacy, sacrifice, and infirmity. White is cold, hard, cruel, and sometimes a symbol of mourning.

Black in many respects is opposed to white. It expresses gloom, darkness, woe, night, death, dread, mystery, horror, terror, evil, wickedness, crime, and mourning.

Gray, one of the black and white series, is less severe than black.

Gray symbolizes humility, melancholy, resolution, solemnity, age, penance, sadness, and mature judgment.

Red, classed as a warm hue, suggests blood, heat, fire, anger, hatred, cruelty, murder, tragedy, shame, and destruction. It can also symbolize power, vigor, health, and passion.

Orange is a warm hue. It is a symbol of autumn, harvest, warmth, plenty, laughter, and contentment.

Yellow is also a warm hue. It suggests heat, liveliness, gaiety, gaudiness, and in some instances cowardice, indecency, decay, deceit, and sickness.

Brown signifies autumn, harvest, plenty, warmth, contentment, and happiness.

Green suggests youth, vigor, spring, immaturity, contemplation, faith, immortality, peace, solitude, life, victory, and sometimes jealousy.

Blue symbolizes coldness, melancholy, the sky, the sea, heaven, hope, constancy, fidelity, serenity, generosity, intelligence, truth, spirituality, and aristocracy. Blue is opposed to its complement, yellow.

Violet signifies sadness, quietness, purity, love, sentimentality, royalty, and wealth.

Purple suggests royalty, heroic virtue, and wealth.

ELEMENTARY ELECTRICITY

CHAPTER 7

INTRODUCTION

This short chapter can hardly prepare one to take an examination for an electrician's license. But even the simplest of outlines for electricity in lighting circuits can help the beginning student of technical practice on the stage to protect himself, his fellow workers, and the equipment they will handle in lighting a play. A better understanding of the principles of this subject will add to the student's confidence and efficiency.

According to contemporary theory, electricity in metallic substances is a flow of electrons, a current in a wire being something like the flow of water in a pipe. It takes pressure to push water through a pipe, this pressure being measured sometimes in pounds per square foot. A current of water can be measured in gallons per minute. Flow of electricity or current might be measured as the number of electrons passing a certain point in an electrical circuit in 1 second. The common unit of current is called an *ampere*. The unit of electrical pressure, or electromotive force, is the *volt*. Carrying the water analogy a bit further, it might be said that a current of water in a pipe encounters a certain amount of friction or resistance to flow, depending on the internal surface of the pipe, its length, and its diameter. A current of electricity in a wire encounters friction, or resistance, depending on the nature of the material of the wire, its length, its diameter, and its temperature. The unit of electrical resistance is the *ohm*.

Conductors and Insulators

The term *conductance* is the antonym of *resistance*. If a substance has high conductivity, it has low resistance. Substances having good conductivity (good conductors) are copper, silver, platinum, mercury, tap water, and aluminum. While aluminum is not as good as copper for conducting electricity, it has been seriously considered as a copper substitute in times of copper shortage. Equivalent aluminum wire would have to be larger in diameter to compensate for its slightly higher resistance. Certain other materials used in electrical equipment that have higher resistances but are still considered conductors are nickel–chromium alloys for resistance dimmers, potentiometers, and heating elements; tungsten wire for incandescent filaments; and carbon for electrical brushes and potentiometers. Insulating materials (essentially nonconductors at ordinary voltages around the theatre) include rubber, paper, porcelain, glass, and many plastics.

OHM'S LAW

There is a simple but very important relationship between the electromotive force (volts), the current (amperes), and the resistance (ohms) in an electrical circuit. This relationship, called *Ohm's law*, which applies to the whole or any part of an electrical circuit, can be expressed in this way. *The electromotive force (e.m.f.) is equal to the product of the current and the resistance.* Using the symbols E for voltage, I for current, and R for resistance,

$$E = IR$$

or
$$I = \frac{E}{R}$$

or
$$R=\frac{E}{I}$$

where I is expressed in amperes, E in volts, and R in ohms.

Example I: Determine the resistance of a lamp which carries a current of 2 amperes flowing under an applied e.m.f. of 110 volts.

$$R=\frac{E}{I}$$

$$R=\frac{110}{2}=55 \text{ ohms, resistance of lamp}$$

Example II: Find the current that will flow through a dimmer or rheostat (see footnotes 1 and 2, p. 118) having a resistance of 25 ohms, if the applied voltage is 125 volts.

$$I=\frac{E}{R}$$

$$I=\frac{125}{25}\quad =5 \text{ amperes, current passing through the dimmer}$$

SERIES AND PARALLEL CIRCUITS

Electrical circuits may be divided into two general classes, series and parallel. All circuits found in practice consist of either series elements, parallel elements, or a combination of the two. A series circuit is one in which the current follows a single path through the several elements, and has the same value in all parts of the circuit (see Figure 7–1).

Problem. Each of the six lamps in Figure 7-1 has a resistance of 10 ohms, and the generator maintains an e.m.f. of 110 volts. Determine the current.

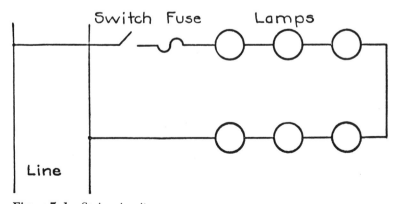

Figure 7–1 Series circuit.

10 ohms per lamp $\times$ 6 = 60 ohms total resistance

$$\frac{E}{R} = I$$

$$\frac{110}{60} = I = 1.83 \text{ amperes, current in the circuit}$$

In a series circuit the applied voltage of the whole circuit is equal to the sum of the voltages across the components of that circuit. We can illustrate this with the same example. Each lamp was assumed to have a resistance of 10 ohms, and a current of 1.83 amperes was found to be flowing through it. Assuming for the moment that we do not know the voltage, let us determine the voltage necessary to maintain that current. The voltage drop across each lamp is, by Ohm's law, $E = IR = 1.83 \times 10 = 18.3$ volts. Adding the voltage drop across each lamp to get the total drop, or the total voltage the generator must maintain, we have six lamps of 18.3 volts each, $6 \times 18.3 = 110$ volts.

The resistance of a series circuit is the sum of the resistances of the components. This was also illustrated in the above example. Six lamps of 10 ohms each possessed a total resistance of 60 ohms. If the connecting wire is long (half a mile, for example), it might have an appreciable resistance that would then be added to the total resistance of the lamps.

A parallel circuit, occasionally called a multiple or shunt circuit, is one whose elements are connected in such a way that the current is divided among the several branches. That is, the current passing from the generator through the circuit and back to the generator will go through as many paths as there are branches in the circuit (Figure 7–2). The parallel circuit is of great importance in theatre lighting, as well as in all interior lighting, because incandescent lamps are commonly connected in parallel.

The voltage across the group of lamps connected in parallel (Figure 7–2) is the same as the voltage across each lamp, provided that the resistance of the connecting wires is so small that it may be neglected. This is certainly true in the usual theatre lighting circuits.

While the resistance of a group of lamps of known wattage can be found by first finding the current with the formula $W = EI$ and then finding the resistance from Ohm's law, there are times when total resistance in parallel is needed directly from the individual resistances. R represents total resistance and r_1, r_2, r_3, and so on represent the individual resistances. Then

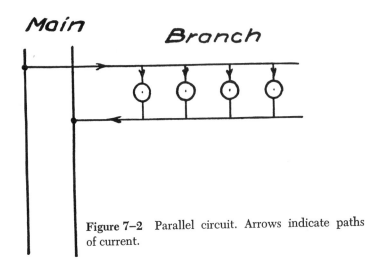

Figure 7–2   Parallel circuit. Arrows indicate paths of current.

$$\frac{1}{R} = \frac{1}{r_1} + \frac{1}{r_2} + \frac{1}{r_3} + \frac{1}{r_4} \cdots$$

Example. $r_1 = 4$ ohms, $r_2 = 6$ ohms, $r_3 = 12$ ohms, $r_4 = 8$ ohms.

$$\frac{1}{R} = \frac{1}{4} + \frac{1}{6} + \frac{1}{12} + \frac{1}{8}$$

$$\frac{1}{R} = \frac{6}{24} + \frac{4}{24} + \frac{2}{24} + \frac{3}{24} = \frac{15}{24} = \frac{1}{R}$$

$$R = \frac{24}{15} = 1\frac{9}{15} \text{ ohms total resistance in parallel}$$

DIRECT AND ALTERNATING CURRENT

Electrical power is produced by batteries such as those in flashlights and motor cars and also by generators such as those in city power plants. The batteries and direct current generators produce current flowing in one direction in a steady stream. This type is rarely found in the theatre except when batteries are used for miniature lamps such as those used in portable candles. For quieter and steadier arc follow spotlights a rectifying device within the base of the instrument converts the usual alternating current into direct current for the carbon arc.

The far more common alternating current of 60 cycles changes direction 120 times a second. If the electromotive force is 120 volts, the pressure rises to 120 volts in one direction, falls to zero, and then rises to 120 volts in the other direction, all within 1 second. For incandescent lighting the change is imperceptible to the human eye because the filament does not have time to cool between the peak voltages.

Much of our electrical equipment, such as transformers to raise and lower voltage and many types of dimmers, including the most common ones, the autotransformer and the SCR, depend on alternating current.

POWER

Power is required to maintain a current of electricity, whether it is direct or alternating. The practical unit of power is the *watt*, the product of volts and amperes.

$$P=EI$$

$$\text{Watts} = \text{volts} \times \text{amperes}$$

Since by Ohm's law $E=IR$, then by substitution $P=I^2R$.

Lamps are rated by the number of watts they consume at a definite voltage.

Example 1. 100 watts at 120 volts. This information, used in the formula $P=EI$, gives the current passing through the lamp. Thus

$$100 = I \times 120 \text{ or } I = \frac{100}{120} = 0.85 \text{ ampere, current through the lamp}$$

With this we are able to determine the resistance of the lamp.

Example 2. What is the resistance of a 1500-watt lamp rated at 110 volts?

$$P=EI$$

$$I = \frac{1500}{110} = 13.\dot{6} \text{ amperes, current through the lamp}$$

Since

$$R = \frac{E}{I}$$

$$R = \frac{110}{13.6} = 8.07 \text{ ohms, resistance of lamp}$$

From these two examples it is clear that the greater the power consumed by a lamp, the greater the current that will flow through it, and the lower will be its resistance.

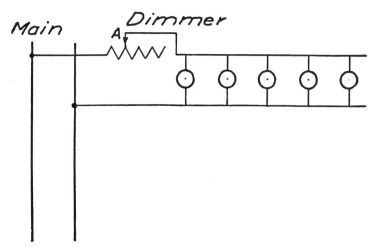

Figure 7–3 Dimmer in series, with group of lamps in parallel.

APPLICATION TO THE STAGE

The problem of changing the intensity of illumination is of fundamental importance in stage lighting. The simplest method of changing intensity is accomplished by placing a *rheostat*[1] (a *dimmer*[2] in the technical language of the theatre) in series with a lamp or groups of lamps (Figure 7–3). When the variable contact is in a position that places the smallest part of the resistance in the circuit, very nearly the maximum current in the circuit is passing the small part of the wire in the rheostat. The resistance wire from which the rheostat is made must be, accordingly, of such size that it will not overheat when the maximum current of the circuit is passing through it. A rheostat is rated in amperes, the maximum current which will not overheat it (it is also rated in ohms, total resistance). Obviously, when a larger part of the wire is included in the circuit, by Ohm's law the current will be proportionately smaller.

In determining the proper rheostat to be employed in a given instance, first one must determine the current in the lamp circuit. This may be done as follows:

Problem. Suppose each of the five lamps in Figure 7–3 has a rating

---

[1] An electrical instrument consisting of an insulated base on which is mounted a length of wire of higher resistance than the usual copper conductor, and having terminals at each end, constitutes an electrical resistance. In cases where the resistance may be varied at will, the device is known as a rheostat.

[2] For a description of a dimmer, a rheostat made expressly for use on the stage, see Chapter 8, pp. 134–135.

of 100 watts at 110 volts, and we wish to know the current-carrying capacity and the resistance of a dimmer capable of dimming these lamps to black.

The total lamp load is

$$5 \times 100 \text{ watts} = 500 \text{ watts}$$

Then by $P = EI$, we have $500 = 110 \, I$ or

$$I = \frac{500}{110} = 4.5 \text{ amperes}$$

This is the amount of current flowing through the line when there is no dimmer in the circuit. Accordingly, for this circuit we select a rheostat or dimmer with a rated capacity of about 4.5 amperes.

The other important consideration is to have sufficient resistance to dim the lamps completely. Knowing the voltage and the current, we can find the total resistance of the lamp load. Thus,

$$R = \frac{E}{I}$$

therefore,

$$R = \frac{110}{4.5} = 24 \text{ ohms (approximately)}$$

It has been determined by experiment that the resistance required to dim a lamp completely is about three times the resistance[3] of the hot lamp load. Multiplying 24 ohms by 3 gives 72 ohms, which is the amount of resistance necessary to dim a lamp load of 500 watts. For this purpose we need a rheostat rated at not less than 4.5 amperes and 72 ohms.

Theatrical dimmers are rated in watts: for example, a 1000-watt dimmer can be safely connected in series with a 1000-watt lamp, or with a group of lamps whose total wattage is 1000. If a larger load were connected to the dimmer, it would overheat and, more than likely, burn out. A smaller load is safe, of course, but a smaller load requires a greater resistance to dim it out completely. For these reasons a resistance dimmer should be connected to a load equal, approximately, to the rating of the dimmer. The discussion and explanation above concerning the current-carrying capacity and resistance necessary for dimming has been included not only to enable the reader to understand the principles involved, but also to serve as a possible guide in the construction of home-made dimmers

---

[3] The resistance of the wire from which lamp filaments are made varies with its temperature. Its resistance is much higher when the lamp is bright than when it is dim.

and in employing rheostats not intended for theatrical use. Producing groups in colleges and high schools can usually borrow rheostats from departments of physics and electrical engineering when the rheostats are to be used for only a day or two. In such cases, a calculation of maximum resistance and current-carrying capacity should always be made to prevent damage to the apparatus. Since resistance dimmers are becoming obsolete, the importance of this discussion lies mainly in helping the reader to understand the electrical circuits.

TRANSFORMERS

A transformer is an alternating current device for changing alternating current voltage to a higher or lower value. It will not work with direct current. It consists of two separate and insulated copper wire coils around a common soft iron core and so arranged that electrical lines of force around one winding will pass through the other by way of the iron core. There is no electrical connection in the usual sense between the two coils of wire (see Figure 7–4). One winding, called the primary, is connected to a source of alternating current. The other winding, which is available to give out energy, is called the secondary. If there are 100 turns of wire in the primary coil and 10 turns in the secondary, it is called a step-down transformer. If 100 volts are applied to the primary, then 10 volts are available at the secondary winding. It can work in the opposite way, with more turns in the secondary and fewer in the primary. Such a transformer is a step-up transformer. Small bell-ringing transformers are made to connect to 120-volt power sources, and the secondary provides 6 volts for a door bell.

For certain applications the primary winding of a transformer does not have to be insulated from the secondary. In fact, the secondary is part of the primary, and two secondary wires lead away from the primary winding. This type can step the voltage up

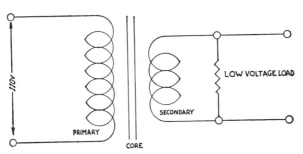

Figure 7–4   Simple step-down transformer.

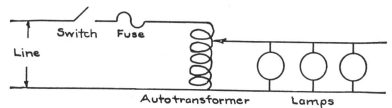

Figure 7–5   Method of connecting an autotransformer.

(usually not much higher than the primary voltage) or down (see Figure 7–5). The autotransformer dimmer, discussed in Chapter 8, is a dimmer operating on this principle. The primary coil, insulated and wrapped around its iron core, has a small portion of each turn of the coil bared so that it may make contact with a sliding device that connects to the lamp or group of lamps to be dimmed. When the slider is at the top of the coil, the 120-volt power goes directly to the lamps, bringing them up to full brightness ("full up"). As the slider is moved down, fewer and fewer turns are connected to the lamps and they are dimmed because the secondary has fewer turns, and accordingly is applying less voltage to the lamps. When the slider is halfway down, the transformer has a step-down two to one ratio of turns producing half-voltage (60), and the lamps are, roughly, half bright.

REACTANCE

If a coil of insulated wire is wrapped around an iron core and designed with the proper number of turns and the right amount of iron in the core, current will tend to flow when the coil is connected to a 120-volt source of energy. Since the core is within the coil, however, there is set up, in the opposite direction, an electromotive force that bucks the original voltage and prevents current from flowing. If lamps are connected in series with this coil, the lamps will be very dim. No voltage remains to push current through their filaments. If the iron core could be removed, the lamps would be bright again. In applying this principle to the dimming of lamps for the stage, it was discovered that a sort of secondary winding could be applied to the same core. The coil becomes a control coil when energized with direct current, and neutralizes the back electromotive force, allowing the normal line voltage to apply a gradually changing alternate current voltage to the lamps as the direct current is varied in the control coil. This makes a very satisfactory dimmer in its present form. At first, direct current generators and

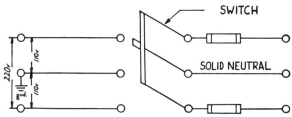

Figure 7–6 A three-wire power system. The rectangles in the top and bottom wires at the right represent cartridge fuses.

large-resistance dimmers had to be added to the control circuit, making the reactance dimmer useful only for very large loads. Later, as explained in Chapter 8, the direct current was supplied by an electronic tube and the same basic reactance dimmer (improved in design) was very good for a remote-control system.

SIMPLE WIRING

Explanations and simple diagrams for connecting lamps in series or in parallel (Figures 7–1 and 7–2) have already been discussed in this chapter. A single resistance dimmer in series with a small group of lamps was shown (Figure 7–3) and discussed, as was an autotransformer (Figure 7–5), in the section above. Electronic, electronic reactance, and magnetic amplifier diagrams are too complicated for this elementary discussion.

THREE-WIRE SYSTEM

Power comes into a building from a transformer on a pole near the street, or from a transformer in a vault in a remote part of a public building such as a theatre. In a metal pipe, called a conduit, a heavy three-wire cable runs to the remote part of a remote-control system or the rear of a direct-control board. As shown in Figure 7–6, the secondary from the transformer, which provides 220 volts between the two outside wires, has a center tap that is called the neutral. From either outside wire to this neutral there will be an elecromotive force of 110 volts. The lines under the *gnd* in Figure 7–6 indicate that this neutral is connected to the ground. By connecting this neutral wire and also the frames and housing of various kinds of electrical equipment, including control boards and spotlights, to the ground, they are made safer for operating personnel. As mentioned in the last chapter under the discussion of electrical cable, city and state electrical codes are being changed to make the

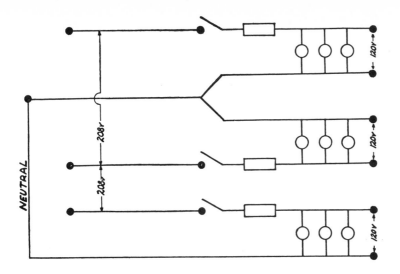

Figure 7–7   Wiring diagram illustrating four-wire, three-phase system.

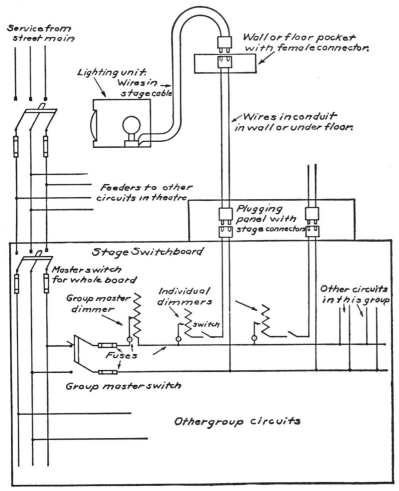

Figure 7–8   Schematic diagram of stage wiring.

grounding of power tools and other electrical equipment required by law.

Figure 7–6 illustrates a single-phase[4] system for lighting circuits. Figure 7–7 illustrates a four-wire, three-phase system that is used where lighting loads are more important than power loads. When this system is used for motors, 208 volts are obtained between any two of the "outside" wires, but lighting loads of 120 volts are connected between any one of the "outside" wires and the fourth, or neutral (grounded), wire.

Figure 7–8 shows three-wire power coming into a lighting control board main switch, and continuing through a group master switch and dimmer that has two individual dimmers and switches going to some type of plugging panel. From here it goes to an outlet where a spotlight with cable is plugged in at the top center of the diagram. At the group master switch two fuses are shown. The more recent practice does not use a second fuse shown in the neutral. As explained in the following chapter under control board parts, in most instances the fuses would be replaced by a circuit breaker and this would be in the "hot" (ungrounded) line only, not in the neutral.

---

[4] If the student is interested in phase or phase relationships, he should refer to any elementary text on electrical engineering.

LIGHTING CONTROL

CHAPTER 8

INTRODUCTION

From the analysis of light and its functions in Chapter 1, and the discussion and description of lighting instruments in Chapter 4, we have seen that instruments cannot, either optically or mechanically, control the properties of light perfectly. Many years ago, David Belasco said, "Without perfect control, lighting in the theatre, instead of being an irresistible means to every end of dramatic effect, would be continuously a hindrance and a stumbling block."[1]

[1] *Theatre Lighting—Past and Present* (Mt. Vernon, N.Y.: Ward Leonard Electric Company, 1928).

Belasco was thinking of the electrical control board where the brightness of each lamp can be changed individually and in a variety of group combinations. Many improvements in instruments and control have been added since the important contributions of Belasco in the early part of the century. What did he mean by "perfect control"? Since light is the medium of expression in the theatre that we know least about, probably we still do not know what perfect control is.

Perfect control seems to be complete control of the properties of light—quantity, color, and distribution—from a single position. From this position the control operator must also be able to see the entire stage and the actors on it. Just as the conductor of an orchestra coordinates the contributions of the individual musical instruments, a lighting control operator coordinates the contribution of each lighting instrument to the whole lighting plan. As in the case of different musical instruments in a symphony orchestra, each lighting instrument is designed and built for a definite purpose and is selected for a specific function in the lighting design of one scene of a play. The lighting control operator has these instruments at his finger tips, bringing them in and out according to the lighting "score." Quantity, color, and distribution may be continually changing.

CONTROL LOCATION

In the many new educational theatres throughout the United States it has become commonplace to locate the lighting control console in the rear of the auditorium. Many new professional theatres in Europe have the lighting console in the same location. Even in New York in the newest theatres one will find the lighting console where the operator has a complete view of the actor and the stage. There has been a slow transition from the old backstage position left or right near the proscenium arch, but this position is still common among older theatres in New York; even throughout the country in theatres and civic auditoriums where traveling productions play for short periods of time, the backstage position for the lighting console is preferred. Portable controls are still an important part of the equipment that is carried by each production. These controls must be connected by flexible cable near the lighting instruments and it is desirable to have any permanent console nearby for good coordination. Good vision seems to be secondary.

In selecting the exact position for the console at the rear of the auditorium, it is desirable to have the console near the center and just above the last row of seats so that the operator has a good view of the lighting on the cyclorama. While the rear of the balcony is far superior to a backstage location, the operator's view of the cyclorama might be only a few feet above the stage floor.

GENERAL CLASSIFICATION—PERMANENT AND FLEXIBLE

There are two methods of lighting control, permanent and flexible. Permanent control is the one in which the wiring from any outlet on the stage, such as the wiring for a borderlight circuit, to a switch and dimmer on the control board, is permanently fixed with no provision for connecting that outlet or instrument to any other circuit on the board. This method of control has developed out of antiquated lighting practice and the associated tradition of equipping theatres with stock lighting instruments, such as footlights, borderlights, and stage pockets for spotlights or floodlights. In the past, these were thought to be the backbone of all stage lighting, and accordingly were always permanently connected to the control board. As a result, in recent years the majority of road companies have carried their own lighting instruments and portable control boards, and have completely ignored the permanent stage lighting equipment in the theatres on the road.

Modern practice in stage lighting requires much more variety and flexibility in an equipment layout, especially for experimental theatres, than the permanent method of control affords. For a number of reasons, then, a method of control has come into use that is far better suited to college, community, and repertory theatres. It is called *flexible control*, which means that between the control board and the outlets where instruments are connected there is some means of connecting any outlet to any dimmer and switch on the control board. Furthermore, any number of outlets can be connected to one dimmer if desirable, as it often is.

INTERCONNECTING PANELS

The device in which connections are made between stage outlets and dimmer controls is called by various names, including interconnecting panel, interconnection panel, interplugging panel, patch panel, and now even programming panel.

The open bus bar type is obsolete because it is illegal, and the rotary type limits the number of dimmers. The plugging types are quite common and satisfactory, but the separable cord variety is objectionable because there must be a place to hang the cords, which tend to get scattered about. The counterweighted fixed-cord

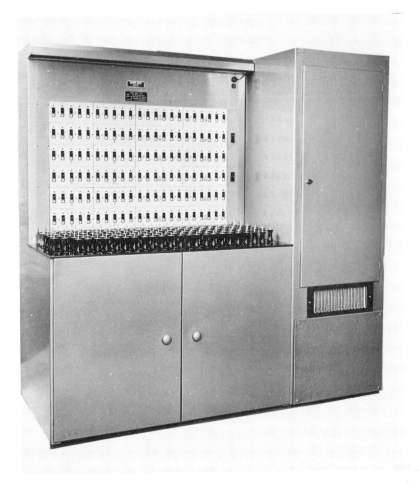

Figure 8–1 Kliegl combination "Safpatch" (automatic cold patch) and SCR Dimmer® bank.

type has one end permanently wired to its individual outlet. A small weighted pulley hangs on the "slack" flexible cord to keep it neatly in place when not in use. See Figure 8–1. The weighted pulley and excess cable to allow the plug to reach any dimmer jack are inside the front portion of the panel. The vertical rear part of the panel contains the dimmer jacks to receive any of the outlet plugs. One disadvantage of the fixed-cord panel is that one must choose a definite maximum of dimmer jacks needed to allow several outlets to be connected to one dimmer. The usual number is six jacks, into which may be plugged six outlets.

The modern slider bus bar type of interconnecting panel shown in Figure 8–2 is completely "dead" front, with only the slider handles

Figure 8–2   Electro Controls (Ariel Davis) Quick-Connect interconnecting
panel.

protruding to the insulated front panel. This type is preferred in two
respects. It extends only a few inches from the stage wall, while
plugging types might be 2 feet or more thick and occupy valuable
stage floor space. The other advantage is that not only can any
outlet be plugged into any dimmer, but also the total number of
outlets, if necessary, can be plugged into any one dimmer. Of course
this is hardly necessary, but in the slider bus bar type one is not
limited to an arbitrary number of dimmer jacks.

The outlet circuit breakers are ordinarily in a panel with a locked
door on the sides of a plugging-type panel and nearby in the slider
type. The slider type is now available for the same price as the
plugging type. A pushbutton type (see Figure 8–3) has been built
but is the most expensive of all.

ADVANTAGES OF FLEXIBLE CONTROL

By means of one of the interconnecting arrangements mentioned
above, flexible control saves time and money and adds to convenience of operation. When connecting instruments to stage outlets, in

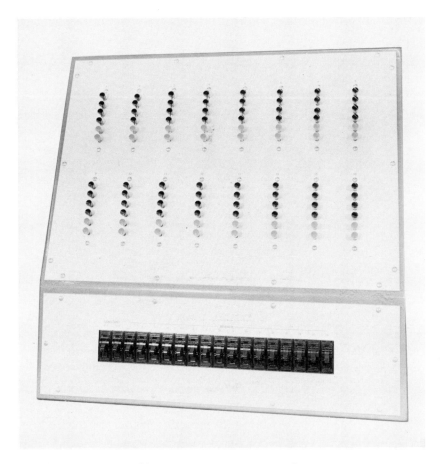

Figure 8–3   Major pushbutton interconnecting panel.

order to conserve stage cable and to avoid excess cable getting in the way of the actors and the shifting scenery, it is necessary to have considerably more stage outlets than are ever needed for one production. These outlets are located in convenient places about the stage so that instruments can be plugged in wherever they are needed. On the other hand, it does not follow that one needs an equal number of dimmer circuits on the control board; in fact, the number of dimmer circuits is often only half the number of outlets, but these figures must be determined by workers in their own theatres who know from considerable experience the actual needs for the sort of plays commonly produced there. The number of dimmer circuits should never be determined by a manufacturer or dealer who thinks he knows what the theatre needs. If the most useful wattages are selected, from 30 to 36 dimmer circuits take care of a fairly elaborate production on a small stage. The number of stage outlets is determined somewhat by the size of the stage, but 60 to 70 is a rough estimate of a convenient number for a small stage. For a medium-size stage there should be between 150 and 200 outlets and from 60 to 100 dimmer controls.

The following advantages are important. In this kind of control, a dimmer of any wattage found on the board (many good ones have dimmers of different wattages) is available to any outlet, and a single dimmer can be connected to two or more outlets, a practice which is frequently necessary. Furthermore, a flexible control board is much cheaper because fewer dimmer circuits are necessary than in permanent control, in which several dimmers may be idle because they are permanently connected to an instrument not in use at the time. Finally, flexible control allows the operator to arrange the controls into groups according to the needs of each production, so that he can handle the switches and dimmer handles with maximum speed and facility and with minimum danger of error.

DIRECT AND REMOTE CONTROL

Control boards are also classified as direct or remote control. In direct control, the switches and dimmers which the operator actually handles carry the total current that passes through the lamps. When a single circuit carries a large group of lamps, or a master switch or dimmer handles the whole board, the space occupied by such a switch or dimmer becomes quite large. Dimming under these circumstances is less subtle and not as smooth as it is with small parts. In remote control the large switches and dimmers are placed in some remote place, such as a basement room, where space is not at a premium. These large parts are controlled by small switches and dimmer handles on a compact pilot console (manually operated control board) out front where the operator can see the entire production.

PRESET OR MULTISCENE CONTROL

For the past 40 years a method of setting up the switches, and later the dimmer readings, for several scenes in advance has been developing. Today it has reached a relatively high state of refinement in contemporary control systems, and is described in the section on memory systems (pp. 150–156) and more elaborately elsewhere.[2] In

[2] See the control board catalogs of the various manufacturers and many articles in periodical literature.

plays with a large number of short scenes with only a few seconds between scenes, it is helpful to have all of the scenes set on the board in advance, up to the intermission of 10 minutes or so, when the operator can set up another group of scenes. Faders are provided on these control boards to change smoothly the individual readings on a group of instruments to another set of dimmer readings on the second preset, and so forth to the last preset available. In the opinion of some, two presets are sufficient, because after one has faded to the second, an assistant can help reset the first preset readings in time for the fade to the third scene, and so on. This argument falls down if the control board has from 50 to 100 individual controls to be reset during a 30-second scene. A representative of the Rank Strand Electric and Engineering Company of London said recently that in England good control boards had at least 144 individual controls. While this sounds like a beautiful dream compared with the average board in an American theatre, it is desirable to have more than the usual 50 to 60 controls commonly found in American theatres. Our controls cost several times as much as those made in England.

So-called *infinite preset* systems have become available in recent years. One system uses IBM-type punched cards that are fed continuously into the system. Another has plastic or aluminum "cards," each with 36 miniature dimmers (see Figure 8–9). The dimmer readings are set in advance and the "cards" are set into the board as needed before the scene begins. The latest "memory"-type lighting control console stores or "memorizes" 500 to 700 cues or readings and brings them into active use as needed (see Figures 8–16 through 8–21).

CONTROL BOARD PARTS

Switches and Protective Devices

A discussion of the way in which control boards operate is difficult without a brief mention of the essential parts of which these boards are composed. The vital essentials for controlling the intensity of an incandescent lamp are a switch to open and close the circuit, a fuse or circuit breaker to guard against short circuits or excessively high current, and a dimmer to change the amount of illumination.

The smallest durable switch which is silent in operation, easy to operate manually, and which meets the requirements of the electrical code is usually the best for stage control boards. Mercury switches are very good but are not common for the stage. Silent mechanical switches seem to be preferred by control board manu-facturers. Toggle switches are much too noisy.

For remote control, a small, compact, silent switch on the pilot console does not carry the full current, nor does it directly energize a large lamp (or lamps) on the stage. It controls a large magnetic switch (contactor) on a control panel in a remote room containing the actual load-carrying switches, fuses, circuit breakers, and dim-mers. This small pilot switch energizes an electromagnet that opens and closes a large switch. In many contemporary control systems the large magnetic switch is not provided in each circuit, but is used only as a blackout switch for a large number of controls, that is, as a master switch for the whole control board. Each no-dim circuit on a remote-control board must have a magnetic switch in the remote portion of the control system. Individual dimmer circuits can be opened or closed without the expense of these magnetic switches by merely opening or closing a part of the control current.

One trend in the last few years has been to have the switches (and dimmers) "back illuminated." This means that each switch has a built-in miniature incandescent (low-voltage) lamp that makes the plastic handle glow when the switch is on. Some glow with different colors to indicate "off," "on," "independent," "master," "individual," and so forth. Back illumination makes it possible to have the ambient illumination at a lower level. Without back illumi-nation it is possible to have ceiling light in the control booth care-fully confined to the console face. In either case the intention is to have adequate illumination for the control operator on the cue sheets, the control handles, and dimmer readings without spilling the light into the nearby auditorium seating.

Either plug or cartridge fuses are satisfactory for stage lighting. The plug type, which screws into place like a lamp, has the advan-tage of displaying the fact that it is either intact or blown. This fuse, however, is not made in sizes above 30 amperes. Cartridge fuses are small cylinders of fiber with brass contacts on the ends. Their size varies with the current to be carried. Circuits should never be overfused; in other words, a circuit carrying current for 500 watts should have a 6-ampere fuse, not a 10-ampere one. The 6-ampere fuse will "blow" if a 1000-watt lamp is connected to a 500-watt dimmer, warning the operator that an overload has been placed on the dimmer; the 10-ampere fuse will not give this warning.

"Slow-blow" fuses are available now and are used in circuits that have current surges. They will withstand a higher current than their rating, but will go out if the higher current is maintained for more than a few seconds.

Small glass cartridge fuses similar to the ones in the electrical systems of motor cars are being used to save space in lighting consoles. They are available in a wide range of ampere ratings.

The circuit breaker, now replacing the fuse in branch circuits (such as individual circuits on a control board), is a thermal device that opens the circuit when excessive current overheats it. This device is provided with a handle to open and close it manually, and a great many models of this type resemble the common toggle switch. Over a period of time the circuit breaker is a good deal cheaper than fuses if the fuses have to be replaced often, and the circuit breaker prevents the dangerous practice of putting pennies behind fuses when they are blown. Either a fuse or a circuit breaker is required by law in each circuit, and anything that interferes with its normal operation is a serious and dangerous matter.

Dimmers

Almost every person actually associated with the production of plays appreciates the supreme importance of being able to change the intensity of light on the stage. Those who need to be convinced are local architects and electrical contractors, school principals and superintendents. The architect and school administrator are often more concerned with combining the cafeteria with the auditorium than they are with making the stage and its equipment effective for producing plays. In 25 years there has been some improvement, but dimming control is neglected all too often.

Dimmers are usually classified according to the electrical principle on which they operate. The ones in use today are resistance, auto-transformer, electronic reactance, electronic, magnetic amplifier, and silicon-controlled rectifier. While resistance dimmers are still in a few very old installations, they are essentially obsolete except for a few portable controls carried by an occasional road company. If there are any theatres left with direct current power (rather unlikely), the resistance dimmer would be the only type that could be used.

Resistance and autotransformer dimmers are essentially direct control in their operation unless they are motor driven. Since a motor drive with variable speed is impracticable, in the opinion of the writer a motor-driven dimmer is unsatisfactory for stage lighting. Electronic, electronic reactance, and magnetic amplifier dimmers are associated with remote control because the dimmers themselves, and their supplementary parts, are rather large and have no moving parts; in this case it is ideal to place them in a place remote from the stage and have the manually operated part of the system, where parts are small and sensitive, in the rear of the auditorium or some other out-front position. Remote-control systems cost from two to three times as much as direct-control systems. For many small schools and colleges a remote-control system is too expensive to consider.

RESISTANCE DIMMERS

In shape, resistance dimmers are either square or round plates, varying in height from about 12 to 20 inches. The round-plate type (Figure 8–4) can be interlocking or noninterlocking. Interlocking means that the handles which change the intensity can be connected in such a way that two or more dimmers set in a row can be operated together by a single handle called the interlocking handle. Figure 8–5 shows how interlocking dimmers (both resistance and autotransformer types) are mounted in rows in a steel frame with a large interlocking handle near the end of each row. These dimmers (if resistance) have 110 steps, so that they will dim very gradually, and each handle is provided with a scale of 10, so that the desired quantity of illumination controlled by the dimmer can be noted and

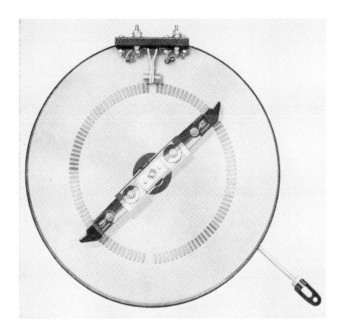

Figure 8–4   Ward Leonard resistance dimmer (interlocking type).

Figure 8–5   Ward Leonard interlocking dimmers. Resistance and autotransformer dimmers can be interlocked in the same way.

recorded for succeeding rehearsals, and for the performance. The noninterlocking dimmers have only about 30 or 40 steps, which does not produce such smooth dimming, and there is no scale provided for noting a dimmer reading. The price of noninterlocking dimmers, however, is only about half that of the interlocking ones. When the most rigid economy must be practiced even at considerable sacrifice in result, the cheaper ones are recommended if used with master dimmers.

Resistance dimmers waste energy in the form of heat, and the load must be fairly closely matched to the capacity of the dimmer. A 500-watt dimmer will not dim out a load smaller than about 450 watts.

Multicapacity Resistance Dimmers

For stage outlets into which spotlights or floodlights of various loads are plugged, dimmers of various ratings are needed. This is taken care of somewhat with a flexible control board, but if the circuits are permanently connected, a multicapacity dimmer is needed. These so-called dual or multicapacity dimmers have, for example, resistance enough to dim a 500-watt lamp and will carry enough current for a 1000-watt lamp.

AUTOTRANSFORMER DIMMERS

Some years ago a new dimmer appeared which used the autotransformer principle that has been common in electrical engineering practice for many years. It consists of a coil of copper wire surrounding an iron core. At one end of its cylindrical form is a dial (much like a large dial of an early model radio), to which is fastened a carbon brush, or sliding contact, which is moved manually around the coil of wire (see diagram in Figure 7–5). In this piece of apparatus there is no heat loss, and practically no energy is used by the dimmer. Its chief advantage, however, is that it has complete variable capacity. That is, a 1000-watt dimmer will dim completely and gradually any wattage, even a 5-watt lamp, up to its maximum capacity (1000 watts).

The large manufacturers of resistance dimmers (and others) soon realized that the autotransformer principle was much superior to resistance for lighting control, and they have designed autotransformers to fit into their standard interlocking frames. The new dimmers are well built and rugged, and have a capacity up to 8000 watts on a single unit. While they have complete variable capacity, they are even more expensive than resistance dimmers, and offer no improvement over these in compactness and subtlety of operation. Autotransformers similar to those in Figure 8–6 are made by the

Figure 8–6   Autotransformer dimmers. Ward Leonard, left; General Radio, right.

large transformer companies also (see the Directory of Manufacturers at the back of the book). Autotransformers operate on alternating current only, whereas resistance dimmers can be used with either direct or alternating current.

Some years ago an autotransformer dimmer that had a number of sliders on a single coil appeared in European theatres. Instead of a coil for every circuit, one coil was provided for every six circuits. This seemed to be a good idea and was later developed in this country by the Ariel Davis Manufacturing Company (now Electro Controls). This Davis dimmer is made in two sizes, 6000 and 12,000 watts, and each has six sliders, any one of which will carry 2500 watts, but of course the total wattage, 6000 or 12,000, must not be exceeded by all six. This unit of control is available with six outlets and circuit breakers to serve as a small portable control board, and also can be combined into groups for stationary installations (Figure 8–7).

ELECTRONIC REACTANCE DIMMERS

As made by the Ward Leonard Electric Company, the electronic reactance dimming circuit consists of the basic reactance coil and

Figure 8–7   Davis dimmer with six sliders.

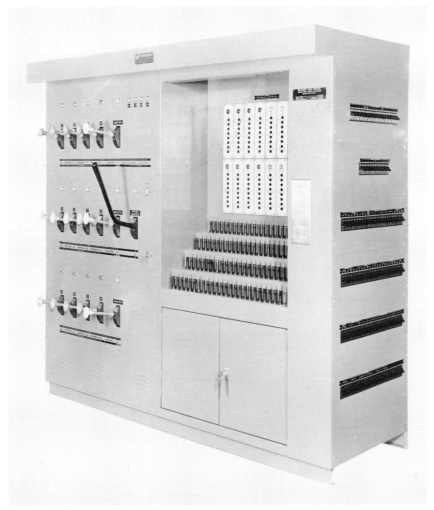

Figure 8–8   Major direct-control board combined with fixed-cord interconnecting panel.

the supplementary controls which they call a Hyster Set. Included are a thyratron electronic tube that produces the direct current, and miscellaneous transformers, potentiometers, and so forth. The reactance coil is in reality two coils, one in series with the lamp to be dimmed, and the other a control coil connected to the direct current produced by the electronic tube. All of this (placed in a remote part of the theatre) is connected by electrical cable to the small manually operated parts on a compact pilot control board (console) placed where the operator can see the stage.

While this type of dimmer is no longer made, it was an improvement over the similar ones made before World War II. The annoying lag or slow response characteristic of large sizes in reactance dimmers of the 1930's was eliminated with the ones manufactured in the late-1940's. The loading range or degree of multicapacity was 80 percent, that is, a 1000-watt dimmer would dim a 200-watt lamp completely. Many of these are still in use, and the consoles had many current features such as preset controls, masters, and submasters.

Figure 8-9 Kliegl "Preset Plate" lighting control console. Two scenes of interchangeable plug-in "preset plates" at right. At left: a system of individual manual controls over the 36 lighting control channels.

ELECTRONIC DIMMERS

An electronic dimmer, developed in the late 1940's, is one in which the large thyratron tubes themselves act as a dimmer, of course with a number of accessory transformers, potentiometers, and so forth. The more elaborate of the two competing electronic control boards, the Century Izenour board, was invented by George Izenour and was manufactured by Century Lighting, Inc. (now Century Strand, Inc.).

The other electronic control board was manufactured by Kliegl Bros. It, too, uses a thyratron-type tube, which actually consists of three tubes in each circuit that serve as the dimmer along with their supplementary parts.

This electronic dimmer was satisfactory in many respects. It would dim any load from 6000 watts down to the smallest lamp. These thyratron tubes produced quite a lot of heat and required good ventilation. While the tubes had a long life, they did burn out and were rather expensive to replace. There are many electronic systems still in use but they are no longer being built.

MAGNETIC AMPLIFIERS

When the magnetic amplifier dimmer (see Figure 8–10) was developed it promised to be the last word in minimum maintenance,

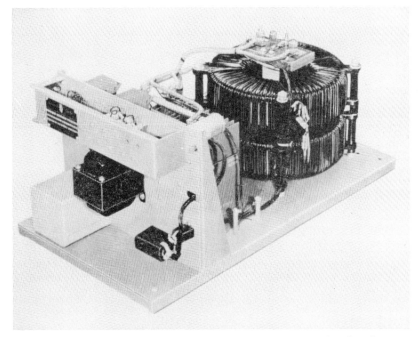

Figure 8–10 Magnetic amplifier type of dimmer. Consoles for this remote-type dimmer can be similar to any of the electronic or electronic reactance consoles.

with no heat problems and no tubes to replace. It had excellent dimming characteristics. This dimmer had reactance coils and dry disc selenium rectifiers, but the circuitry was quite different from that in the reactance dimmer. It would dim any load from its rated capacity down to one-thirtieth of that amount. It was made in sizes from 2000 watts to 25,000 watts, so while it was expensive it was the only dimmer available in larger sizes until recently. The magnetic amplifier was also heavy and bulky, and now it cannot compete with the latest development.

SILICON-CONTROLLED RECTIFIERS

In recent years a new dimmer called a *silicon-controlled rectifier* (SCR) has taken the place of all of the others mentioned above for remote control. Two of these solid-state semiconductors are used, one for each half of the sine wave in an alternating current. This dimmer is manually controlled by a potentiometer in a low voltage (24-volt) circuit on the console. Since this is a very sensitive device, it needs such protective devices as an "amp trap," a circuit-opening device that operates much faster than a common fuse or circuit breaker. A reactor-type "choke" is part of the circuit to prevent surges such as the one that occurs when an incandescent lamp is turned on. Another protection is to use an oversized SCR. Another part of the circuitry is a "feedback" network to give the desired dimming curve, which can be adjusted with three potentiometers when the dimmers are installed. The curve generally agreed upon by lighting directors and manufacturers is called the *square law curve*. For example, when the dimmer reading is 5, the illumination is 25 percent. When the reading is 8, the illumination is 64 percent. The potentiometers also allow one to adjust the minimum so that the lamp filaments are black and the maximum can be set to provide the voltage the lamps are made for, or some variation of this as the theatre lighting director may desire. The load will dim completely 1 percent of the dimmer rating. They are made in sizes from 3000 watts to 12,000 watts. Other sizes can be ordered. SCR's have a metallic heat dissipator called a heat sink and will operate in an ambient temperature of 40°C.

Each of the well-known manufacturers, including Kliegl, Century Strand, Ward Leonard, Skirpan, and the Davis Division of Electro Controls, manufactures its version of the SCR dimmer with slightly different circuitry but with custom-made consoles composed of each company's individual parts.

Because these systems, including the SCR and the console controls, are fairly expensive, each of these companies carries a cheaper line of SCR dimmers with "portable" manually operated units of control with another "package" of the portable dimmers that can be placed nearby or in some remote location. The manual controls are cheaper and the actual dimmers are sometimes not as well protected; usually, they do not have the "curve" or dimming characteristics equal to the more expensive line.

MASTER DIMMERS

One hand with a master dimmer can do more than a dozen hands using individual dimmers. If the individual dimmers can be interlocked, it is true that one hand will serve to dim them all at once, but interlocking requires a much greater pull, and accordingly affords less smooth and subtle dimming. The real advantage that justifies the expense of a master dimmer is something called *proportional dimming*. Suppose a master dimmer is connected (electrically) to four individual dimmers, with dimmer readings of each at full up (that is 10, on a scale of 10), 7, 5, and 2. By changing the handle of the master only, all four individuals will begin dimming at the same time, and all will dim out at the same time. The relative inten-

Figure 8–11   Skirpan Lighting Control Corp., five-preset, 36-channel control console assembled with standard relay rack consoles and modular control panels. (Photo courtesy Frank Bauer.)

Figure 8–12   California State Theatre, California State University, San Diego, lighting control and preset (five) boards by Century Strand with dimmers by Ward Leonard. (Photo courtesy California State University, San Diego, Audio-Visual Services.)

sities of the four lamps will be the same whether the master is at 10 or 5 or any other setting. This is called *proportional dimming,* an important element in control board planning and design. A group master is useful for dimming a smaller group, such as one consisting of six anteproscenium spotlights that go up as the curtain goes up. Another group master may dim an entire sky consisting of five or six different circuits controlling three colors in the cyclorama base lights, and light and dark blue groups of floodlights for the upper part of the cyclorama. When dimming down a late afternoon sky, unity and proportion must be kept in mind. And last, a whole group of area instruments must be able to go up or down when an actor pushes a wall switch button, which may be a cue for the grand master, leaving only a few instruments constant for backings and sky.

Although master dimmers for direct control are quite expensive because their size must be equal to the total load connected to them, in remote control the matter is much simpler and the cost very little beyond that of the individual controls. In mastering remote controls, the master dimmer is only mastering the small individual pilot controls on the manually operated console, and may consist of a small autotransformer or variable resistance carrying a very small current like that in all of the parts on the console. No additional parts need to be added to the heavy remote equipment.

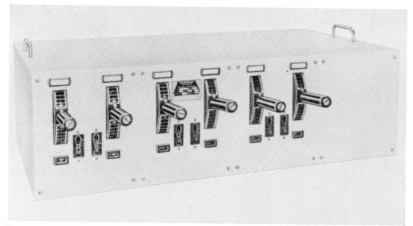

Figure 8–13   Superior Electric Co.'s portable "package" dimmers of the autotransformer type.

PORTABLE CONTROL BOARDS

A portable control board is what its name implies—a control board
light enough to be either carried about by hand or rolled on casters.
It consists of the usual parts associated with stationary boards—
dimmers, switches, circuit breakers, wiring, outlets, and sometimes
an interconnecting panel. Almost any stage lighting equipment
manufacturer will make control boards of the portable variety
according to the customer's specifications or can provide certain
stock sections. Many theatre groups buy parts and assemble their
own portable controls. While the basic function of such a board, by
definition, is control that is portable, this type of equipment appeals
also to those seeking lighting control that is reasonable in price.

Theatre groups starting with little equipment have accumulated
dimmers in small numbers and have assembled them in boxes of
wood or steel, planning to add more dimmers later. Both the Ward
Leonard Electric Company and the Superior Electric Co. have
"packaged dimmer" units, illustrated in Figure 8–13, in standard
"packages" of three, four, five, and six dimmers of the autotransformer type, including circuit breakers, switches, and outlets for
plugging lighting instruments directly into the portable board. An
older type assembled by Century Strand Inc., for the professional
theatre is illustrated in Figure 8–14. An interesting variation built
by Electro Controls is intended particularly for schools and colleges. Such a portable dimmer was discussed on page 138. It was
mentioned earlier in the chapter that most theatrical producers in
New York rent portable control boards. Many such pieces of control

Figure 8–14 Century Strand portable control boards of older type.

equipment are used in television studios, particularly in New York City.

CONTROL BOARD DESIGN

There are several fundamental questions involved in planning a lighting system for a theatre old or new. The answers depend somewhat on the personality and personnel of the theatre organization. If the artists in the theatre work well together, they usually develop a group personality and philosophy of production. This could be true even if the group is composed of just two people. A college group will have a different philosophy from a community group. A theatre organization in a large university in a small community will have a different point of view from that of a similar organization in a college in a large city. The important thing to remember is that attitudes and production methods vary considerably from group to group, and they should be reflected in the planning of lighting control.

It goes without saying that one should have flexible control that requires an interconnecting panel. A large stage requires a large number of outlets, perhaps 100 to 200; a medium-size stage could use 80 to 150, and a small one, 40 to 80.

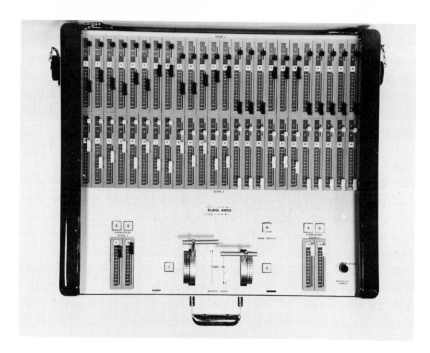

Figure 8–15   Kliegl suitcase remote-control lighting console. Twenty-four Scene 1 potentiometers at top, each with submaster A and B and off switching. Scene 2 below. At bottom: submasters for Scene 1, the split fader, and submasters for Scene 2. All of these controls utilize pushbutton-type blackout switches with SCR dimmers.

The number and type of dimmers is a more difficult decision. For a large stage and a liberal budget, remote control using SCR-type dimmers is preferred. In any case it would be better to have about 100 individual dimmer controls, with about half of the dimmers of 6000 and 12,000 watts and half of them of 3000 watts.

A medium-size theatre should have 48 to 64 individual control circuits of about the same wattages. A small theatre needs a minimum of 30 to 36 individual controls, but more would be better if its staff prefers elaborate productions. Wattages can be somewhat smaller for this theatre; perhaps six dimmers of 4000 or 6000 watts each, and the rest of 2000 watts would be satisfactory. If, for reasons of economy, the demand is for direct control, the autotransformer is the type of dimmer to specify; and the best wattages would be 6000, with a saving in cost possible if half of the dimmers are 2000 or 3000 watts.

A modern control board should be arranged in the simplest possible way that conforms to present-day lighting practices. Furthermore, there are certain limiting factors, such as the reach of the average person's arm as he sits in front of a console. The space between controls should be suited to the anatomy of the hand, and the space between rows of handles should be such that minute changes in the dimmers can be done with the hand resting as the fingers move the controls. The phone should be within easy reach and a headset phone is desirable. A clock either built into the board or near it is very useful.

A flexible system with an interconnecting panel makes it possible to arrange the board, to a degree at least, in the best way for each production. Some people feel that this is confusing, but when students are learning, the operator or operators are usually new for each production.

If the operator sits at the center of the controls so that he can reach in both directions, it seems reasonable to place the master controls in the center of the console (see the section on master dimmers). In a remote system, master controls are relatively simple and do not add greatly to the expense. In a direct-control system, the master dimmers have to be very large, equal in wattage to the sum of the individual dimmer wattages. For example, if there are 24 2000-watt individual autotransformer dimmers, there should be four 12,000-watt group master dimmers that would have to be remote-control 12,000-watt SCR's. For a single grand or system master a fifth control can be added, not another remote dimmer. This provides direct control of individual dimmers and remote control for the masters. In this case the "console" would probably be arranged in four groups of six individual dimmers with the group and grand masters in the center. This arrangement could be increased to 36 individual direct controls, six group or submasters, and a grand or system master (remote control) without becoming too large or clumsy.

Keeping in mind the relationship of the arrangement of the face of the console and the lighting of the play as a whole, the size of each group is important. The six individual dimmers in a group are related to the six spotlights commonly distributed over the upstage or downstage areas. Referring to the description of area lighting in Chapter 9, one can see how the six basic acting areas can be lighted and controlled by two groups of six dimmers, one above the other, arranged on the console as they are on the stage (upstage and downstage). With a larger number of dimmers, say 32, one might have four groups of eight, adding to the basic six instruments two special instruments controlled by the two extra controls in the group. If one is doing a play requiring a higher proportion of special instruments, an arrangement can be made whereby six basic instruments in one group are supplemented by six specials, each placed just below or above the specific place on the control board to which it relates. From these examples one can see how certain divisions into groups, along with the opportunities of change through the patch panel, can connect the planning of the console with the planning of the lighted areas. Light coming from the right (stage right) to the right side of the stage would be connected to dimmers on the same side (left) of the console out front.

The planning of the individual control unit is important too. It will always have an off-on switch, and usually a three-position (individual-master-preset) switch. The latter allows one to remove one or more individual circuits from the preset or master dimmer and allows it to remain constant while others are being dimmed by the master. If the board is not of the multiscene type (see p. 131), the individual control will probably have nothing more than one dimmer, one switch, and a pilot light. The pilot light indicates to the operator at a glance whether the circuit is one or off. If this is a multiscene board there will be a dimmer handle (and sometimes a switch) for each scene.

In the central section of the console one usually finds a grand master control (with switch), a scene master control for each scene, and, if there are more than two scenes, a fader to dim from one scene to another is desirable. A blackout switch that will throw all of the controls on or off instantly is a standard part of every console.

There are many variations of the general plan suggested here. Whether there are preset dimmers or not it is very useful to have group or submaster dimming controls (remote control) for each group of from six to ten individual dimmers. In recent years there has been a trend toward having a console with all of the individual dimmers in line across the width of the board, if the number of individual dimmers is not greater than about 64, with group masters near the groups they control. Grand master, scene masters, and fader can be above or below (see Figure 8–12). The preset dimmers are frequently on a separate console or split into two "wings" flank-ing the main console. An assistant operator can be assigned to the preset console. Switches should be placed logically near the dimmers they control. An off-on switch and a three-position switch—"preset," "master," and "individual"—and the dimmer make up a unit of con-trol. Back illumination of switches and dimmers was discussed on p. 133. A place for the script and/or cue sheets should be included with proper illumination.

"MEMORY" SYSTEMS

The trend in lighting control systems seems to be toward computer or "memory" systems in which cue and preset information can be stored—if one can afford it. These systems offered by Kliegl, Strand, Electro Controls, Skirpan, and Century Strand (and perhaps others) are the most compact, relatively simple and versatile of them all and, of course, the most expensive.

The actual dimmers are silicon-controlled rectifiers, the same device used in all contemporary control systems. Each of these well-known companies has its own circuitry and each has developed a rugged, reliable dimmer that has now stood the test of several years of operation and minor improvements. Each one produces dimming characteristics, such as the square law curve, that meet the demands of the trade.

The latest development, the computer or memory system, consists essentially of three basic parts—the dimmer bank (usually SCR's as mentioned above), the computer or memory "bank," and the console. The first two do not vary much from one manufacturer to another, but the consoles vary considerably and some can be custom-made to incorporate the ideas of the purchaser.

Figure 8–16   Electro Controls memory-type console.

The heart of the system is the ability to store several hundred cues or preset scenes, greatly extending the typical five- or ten-scene control console of a few years ago. Each of these consoles includes group masters, scene masters, grand masters, and cross-fading controllers to any degree of complexity desired. Some of them have a complete set of "rehearsal" or individual dimmer controls on the console, while others recommend a smaller number of "channel" controls, each with an "intensity indicator" where any one or a number of stored readings can be instantly flashed at will. Some consoles can flash only one reading at a time. It is the writer's opinion that a complete set of readings, one for each dimmer in a particular scene, should be available with one flash. This is more expensive because it requires a controller and indicator for each dimmer in the system. The console would be a bit larger too, but it would save much set-up and check-out time.

In many respects, this is a big improvement of the common preset or multiscene system, but it will definitely cost more at present. The prices of the old and new systems come closer together as the total number of dimmers and the complexity of the console increase. Figures 8–16 through 8–20 show variations among several manufacturers.

Several other control manufacturers have somewhat similar memory control systems, each with its own special features. Century

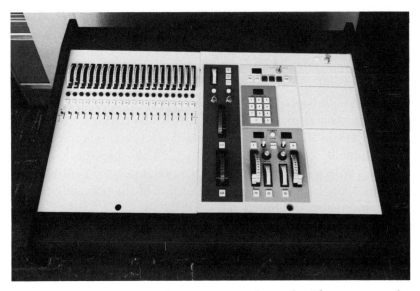

Figure 8–17   Century Strand Memo-Q control console. (Photo courtesy George A. Bahrman Studio.)

Figure 8–18　Rank Strand DDM console with rocker tablet controls for 240 channels on the wing at left. (Photo courtesy Graphoto Studios Ltd.)

Strand has Memo-Q, developed in Los Angeles (see Figure 8–17) and also a newer and more expensive one developed in London by Mr. Frederick Bentham called Rank Strand System DDM, illustrated in Figure 8–18. The latter has a small console and a wing panel with individual "rocker tablet" controls for each dimmer. The Rank Strand DDM is said to lend itself more to custom variations than the Memo-Q. The Skirpan Lighting Control Corp. has brought out a new AutoCue Memory System invented by Mr. Adrian B. Ehlinger and illustrated in Figure 8–21. This system uses standard computer parts and plug-in elements. It can be custom-made to suit individual needs and features a standard television monitor displaying a complete set of dimmer readings. This monitor is used in connection with a "light pen." When the pen is pressed gently against the monitor, the computer reads the position of the pen and performs the appropriate control function.

One of the latest memory systems, called Q-file, was designed by Thorn Lighting of England and is being distributed in the United States by Kliegl Bros. It is illustrated in Figures 8–19 and 8–20. This system consists of a small console of about 3 square feet in area, a memory bank with no moving parts, and a dimmer bank of SCR's. Such dimmers, manufactured by any of the well-known dimmer manufacturers, are compatible with this new system. One of the criticisms leveled at earlier memory systems was that they were not entirely reliable. After 30 installations of Q-file there is evidence of a very high level of reliability as well as of great flexibility and versatility.

While it is almost impossible to describe completely the operation of the console illustrated in Figures 8–19 and 8–20, with the many possibilities of variety in its functions, it seems essential that an attempt should be made. Seeing it in operation or actually handling the controls themselves would add much to the students' understanding. Until this opportunity arises, perhaps the following comments are in order.

Figure 8–19 shows Q-file's typical arrangement of pushbutton and fading controls; the white numbers in the black circles have been added to designate the specific part being discussed and described. At left, is a manual master to control all of the dimmers in use at any one time, but it is hardly needed with all of the other fading devices. At right, is a group of pushbuttons, one combination for each dimmer such as dimmer number 99 at the top. When buttons are pressed for a certain dimmer, the dimmer handle (far right) can be set at a specific reading. At any time later when that dimmer's buttons are pressed, a servo-controlled fader with 80 discreet steps moves the dimmer handle (far right) to the reading previously selected. To turn that dimmer on and energize the instrument connected to it, one presses stage button (left center). The operator or lighting designer continues to turn on all of the needed

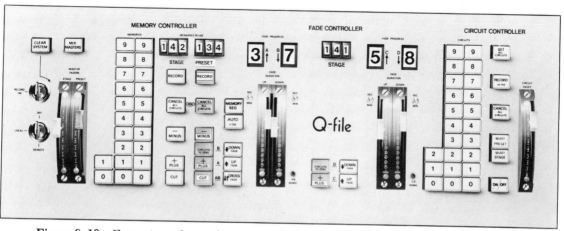

Figure 8–19   Face view of complete operational control panel for the Kliegl Q-file memory lighting control system. Size approximately 34 inches × 11 inches. (Courtesy Kliegl Bros.)

Figure 8–20   Q-file Lighting Control Console. This size console controls up to 360 dimmers with 100 or 200 memory positions. Operational controls left in front of operator. Auxiliary manual "bypass" controls to operator's right. At top of desk panel light shows dimmers energized on stage and in preset. (Courtesy Kliegl Bros.)

instruments by pushing appropriate buttons (right) and selecting a dimmer reading for each instrument by using circuit fader or dimmer (far right). When he has a group of instrument (and dimmer readings) established as a cue or preset group, he stores the readings in the memory section (numbered push button left), where 200 cues or presets can be stored and recalled instantly as needed.

The center section of the console includes the fade controllers. With these faders one can fade or cross-fade from one cut or preset to any other cut or preset. By having four (two up and two down) fade controllers, one can have four groups fading at different speeds or fades within fades. These faders are timing devices that can be set for any time between 1 and 70 seconds or between 1 and 70 minutes. The operator initiates the fade and can revise its speed at any time during a fade. The large numbers above the fader controllers show the percentage progress of the fade.

It would be complicated to describe the multitude of possibilities that are available to the lighting designer with this Q-file system. It is obvious, perhaps, that it is unnecessary to write down all of the dimmer readings for each cue or scene with these memory systems because they are stored within the memory bank. In a repertory theatre doing several plays each week it might be desirable to have a supplementary unit that would record the memory readings for each play on a cassette tape to save time in resetting the console for each play.

Figure 8–21   Skirpan Lighting Control Corp. AutoCue Control Console with 120 channels displayed. (Photo courtesy Oscar & Associates, Inc.)

Figure 8–20 shows a frosted glass panel in the upper left section where the cue number is flashed as that cue is added to the suquence.

This new system is being discussed in the stage lighting world with much enthusiasm and promises to be a landmark in the progress of control.

Since a control board is an expensive item in any list of stage equipment, the planning of it should be given a great deal of thought and discussion. The representatives of the better manufacturers are helpful in discussing various types and possibilities and even in writing specifications. Sometimes completely unbiased advice is needed. The suggestions here are intended to be an outline for the student and a guide for those considering the purchase of new control equipment. Such memory systems of lighting control can definitely help improve the aesthetics of stage lighting.

LIGHTING PRACTICE

CHAPTER 9

INTRODUCTION

The preceding chapters have presented an analysis of the philosophy
of light in the theatre, a short history, a survey of light-producing
instruments and their accessories, the fundamentals and the application of color, and the methods and equipment of lighting control.
This chapter is concerned with the application of these things in
lighting plays, both in general practice and in specific productions.
In the discussion of specific instruments, their various uses have
been mentioned. Here these suggestions will be gathered together
in review and in elaboration to complete the story of lighting on
the stage.

157

When a lighting director approaches the design in light for a specific production, he can think of filling a three-dimensional space with light. Adolphe Appia said, "Light is to space what sounds are to time—the perfect expression of life."[1] Light defines and limits space for the actor and audience. It may be a complex three-dimensional composition, a design created by shafts and pools of light in space. The visible space is limited also by the size of the stage, the width and height of the proscenium opening, and in many situations by certain scenic elements. This space, of course, is selected by the demands of the plays, the stage director, and the scenic designer. The director and designer must agree on a ground plan including floor space, steps, levels, and platform areas above the stage floor where the actors will move from time to time.

THE BALANCE OF ILLUMINATION

The effective lighting of any play or scene depends upon a properly proportioned mixture of two kinds of illumination, general and specific. As was mentioned in Chapter 1, specific illumination brings variety to the stage, and because it is shadow producing, it is also form revealing. In contrast to this, general illumination softens shade and shadow, modifies excessive contrasts in specific illumination, and creates the general color tonality of the whole area.

Lighting the Actors Face

When lighting a play, the lighting director must not forget that his first duty is to the actor. If the actor is not lighted effectively, he is not being supported and reinforced in his effort to interpret the play for an audience. When one is concerned with the coordination of scenery and lighting, of instrument placement in relationship to the scenic elements in the ground plan, and in the cooperative efforts to share limited space, it is easy for him to forget that in lighting the acting area, the actor comes before the background.

A set of photographs (Figure 9–1, a through h) was made to call attention to the simplest matters concerned with lighting the actor's face. Figure 9–1(a) shows the face reduced to a skull-like appearance by a spotlight directly overhead. Figure 9–1(b) is the same, with footlights added. By partly illuminating the eyes, the results is an emaciated or gaunt expression. In Figure 9–1(c), with foot-

---

[1] Adolphe Appia, *The Work of Living Art,* translated by H. D. Albright (Coral Gables, Fla.: University of Miami Press, 1960).

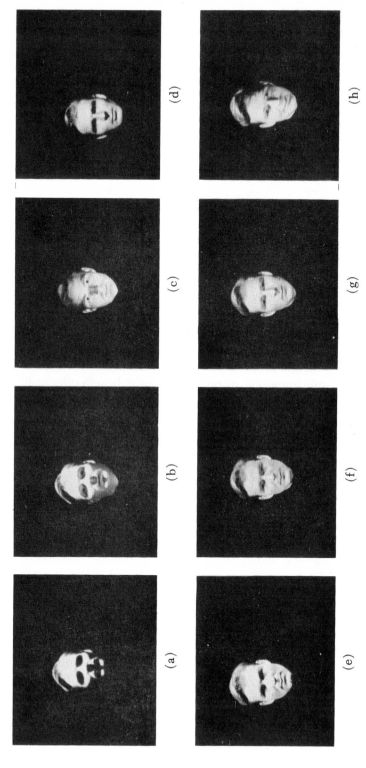

Figure 9–1 (a) Spotlight directly above. (b) Same as (a) with footlights added. (c) Footlights alone. (d) Spotlight 45° above horizon and directly in front. (e) Two spotlights in front, 60° apart and 45° above horizon. (f) Same as (e) but footlights added to improve eyes. (g) Same as (f) with 75 percent more footlights. (h) Same as (e) but with one spotlight turned off.

lights alone, the shadows are reversed from the usual direction and a surprised but not unpleasant expression results. In Figure 9–1(d) a rather hard or severe look is achieved by a single spotlight about 45° above the horizontal, and directly in front. Notice the dark frame of shadow on the sides of the face. The right ear looks detached. In Figure 9–1(e) the face is lighted by two spotlights at a vertical angle of 45°. The horizontal angle between them is about 60°. This is more effective, but the eyes are too dark to be expressive. The face lighting is improved in Figure 9–1(f) by the addition of footlights that bring out the eyes. By adding more footlight illumination in Figure 9–1(g), face shadows are wiped out to the extent that a rather bland, naïve expression is the result. Figure 9–1(h), with footlights and a spotlight from one side, is interesting for a static pose, but too much is lost when the actor moves. If the actor were static, like a piece of sculpture, lighting him effectively would be comparatively simple. After studying a static pose, one would place a source of specific illumination at that ideal horizontal and vertical angle which would cause areas of shade and shadow to contrast most effectively with highlights. Then one would add general illumination of just the right amount to soften the contrast between highlight, shade, and shadow and to produce a desirable color tonality in the areas of less illumination. In this way, a single actor remaining immobile in one area might be effectively lighted; but alas, the problem is not so simple. The actor is in almost constant movement within an area, and he ordinarily uses all of the areas in a setting. Thus a degree of complexity is introduced.

THE ACTING AREAS

The total acting area varies in size and shape from play to play, and it is usually subdivided into smaller areas by the director and lighting director to allocate space to specific scenes in the play under consideration. Variety in the use of areas is highly important in the planning of business and movement of a production. This is especially true in a one-set production, where changes of scenery cannot help provide variety in form and area. Here the lighting director can assist the director in the selection of areas of different sizes and shapes controlled in quantity, color, and distribution to make these areas seem new each time they are used. Thus the lighting director becomes a collaborator with the scene designer and director in the best interest of an exciting and effective production.

On a small to medium-size stage with a proscenium opening of 20 to 28 feet, the usual division is into the six common areas that all

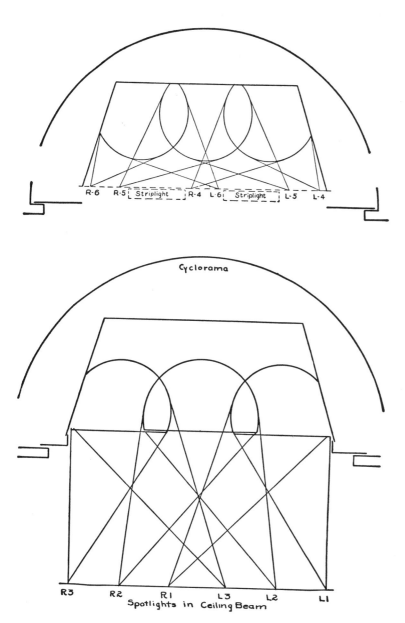

Figure 9–2   Diagram of general lighting plan.

directors and actors call down left, down center, down right, up left, up center, and up right. It is fairly common to have the upstage areas a little less wide than the downstage areas and many irregular ground plans may eliminate an upstage area or add a seventh or even an eighth area farther upstage. Balconies, landings, and additional rooms directly behind the main room may require additional areas.

On a larger stage with an opening of 30 to 36 feet there could easily be a need for four or five areas at the curtain line as far as lighting is concerned and more than three areas in width farther upstage. If the selection of acting area instruments (spotlights) is limited, the areas might have to be increased in number because the available instruments are too narrow beamed for an area of larger diameter.

For open-stage productions the stage area may be enclosed by some sort of cyclorama. In this case the actual acting space would be somewhat smaller, limited in width by sight lines and in depth perhaps by acoustical considerations. Many theatres have a forestage of considerable area in front of the proscenium. This varies in depth and is often wider than the proscenium opening.

In many newer theatres (and some older ones) the forestage and the downstage areas are lighted from auditorium ceiling ports commonly called beams or anteproscenium positions. Hopefully, such openings are as wide as the auditorium ceiling and at a distance from the proscenium arch that will allow a vertical lighting angle of about 45°. Experience tells us that this is a good vertical angle to light the actor's face. A much higher angle will give the actor black shadows in his eye sockets and under the nose and chin. For such a case some sort of "fill" light will be needed from footlights or from another source at a lower angle. If the vertical angle (from the high light or key) is too low, like that from a balcony front position, the actor will have a flatter appearance.

For purposes of lighting, an area is usually 7 to 10 feet wide, and one should think of this area as being not on the floor but at the level of the actor's head. Areas produced by some ellipsoidal spotlights have a shape based on the square (from framing shutters) and those from the Fresnel spotlight are elliptical in shape.[2] While it is possible to light an area with a single spotlight, at least two and sometimes more will do a far better job, because the actor is in motion turning from one side to the other roughly about 180° to the audience. Even if he were a statue a single instrument would not

---

[2] Depending on the vertical angle to the floor.

produce both key and fill, general and specific illumination, highlight and partly illuminated shade and shadow to contribute to character and expression. Ordinarily, two spotlights providing light at vertical angles of about 45° with about 90° between them do an adequate job. There are, however, a number of exceptions involving scenic forms, color changes, and other physical matters.

In any theatre the anteproscenium instruments should be ellipsoidal spotlights. A conventional spotlight with a plano-convex lens will serve, but its efficiency is about 8 to 10 percent compared with the ellipsoidal efficiency of 25 to 30 percent. The conventional spotlight with the Fresnel lens is unsatisfactory for the anteproscenium position because its spill light outside its direct beam will illuminate the teaser and auditorium walls. The wattage needed for each instrument depends on the length of throw. In a small theatre with an anteproscenium throw of about 20 feet or less, one needs a 6-inch lens ellipsoidal spotlight with either a 500- or 750-watt lamp. If the throw is about 30 feet, an 8-inch lens ellipsoidal spotlight with a 1000-watt lamp is needed. For a throw of about 40 feet, one can use a 10-inch lens ellipsoidal with a 1000- or 1500-watt lamp. Notice that the larger the diameter of the lens in an ellipsoidal spotlight, the narrower the beam. If the areas are about the same in diameter the right selection of instrument for a particular distance allows one to keep the framing shutters almost wide open. Thus one is getting the most from each instrument. For four downstage areas, then, in a proscenium opening of about 36 feet one would use eight 8-inch ellipsoidal spotlights.

These eight downstage area instruments should always be connected to eight individual dimmer circuits, one dimmer for one spotlight. If there are absolutely no dimmers available for this purpose when the whole pattern or design for the play is calculated, there are two makeshift substitutions that can be considered. One can use four dimmers instead of .eight, one dimmer for each area, allowing no variety in brightness from the two directions (except two different wattages if desired) and no opportunity for a difference in color from the two directions. Another alternative is to use one dimmer for the left spotlights and one for the right ones, controlling direction, brightness, and possibly color but losing area control. These two alternatives are better than no control when one is limited to a total of about 24 dimmers.

Returning to the preferred control of each spotlight, the advantages and possibilities will soon be evident. By keeping the brightness of one side of the actor higher than the other one can achieve a key light from one direction and a fill light from the other. This balance can be reversed from time to time as the scene demands and as the emphasis shifts. If the lighting designer is using warm light from one direction and cool from the other he might shift the key light from warm to cool or vice versa as the mood of the scene or play changes, or if a different time of day calls for a different lighting distribution.

There are times when a variation in color on each side is not indicated. A different color on each side of the face may distort the make-up, or the costume may look very strange with two different colors of light. When a conventional interior set is used, one area instrument may not fall on the side wall but the other direction may light the wall 6 or 7 feet up from the floor. On the opposite side wall, the area instrument with the other color will spill up on the wall. The two walls may look as if they belonged to two different sets of scenery instead of one. Here a single color is preferred.

Lighted areas must overlap, partly to prevent the actor from walking through or even stopping in a "dark" place between areas. This overlapping must not be carried too far or a monotonous flat appearance will result. In using four areas across the stage instead of three, the very center line of the stage will be lighted by the overlap of areas 2 and 3. For the actor who loves the exact center, or the director who blocks him there, a special instrument may be needed to increase the lighting level in this area.

The upstage areas, three, four or even more, are lighted in a similar manner with horizontal angles about the same, approximately 90°. Vertical angle will vary with the teaser height, since the teaser must mask these instruments from the front row whether they are mounted on a bridge or a teaser batten. Footlights, in addition to illuminating eye sockets, help in blending, but they are rarely used in contemporary lighting practice.

In addition to the area instruments, special instruments are needed to light doorways, archways, and stairways. Ordinarily, upstage area instruments are not focused high enough to light an actor as he stands in the door frame. This requires a special instrument, preferably an ellipsoidal spotlight, because the framing shutters can confine the beam to the exact opening. For that matter, any part of the stage may require a special instrument to build up the light for a particular scene. Perhaps it is desirable to dim down the areas and keep a special or a different color at a higher level. Specials might also be mounted in the anteproscenium position.

To separate the actor from the background, spotlights are sometimes mounted directly overhead on a batten 2 or 3 feet upstage of the first pipe. Their beams are directed straight down to highlight hair and shoulders. This is called "rim" lighting.

Another way to help separate the actor is by back lighting if the stage is open without a ceiling. These instruments are placed on a batten farther upstage and should not be allowed to spill their light outside of the curtain line. Both of these angles help in the form-revealing function of light and make the actor seem more important.

MOTIVATIONS FOR ACTING AREA LIGHTING

When interiors appear to be illuminated by artificial light from floor lamps, table lamps, candles, and other sources of very low intensity in themselves, they serve as motivation for area instruments of greater illumination and variation in color. Exterior motivations, such as sunlight, can be produced by spotlights or special instruments producing parallel rays. These may add to the visibility at times, but they are useful chiefly to produce highlights and to justify the use of certain colors and higher levels of illumination in certain places on the acting area. In this way such sources of light accomplish several functions at the same time.

All visible sources of light, such as table and floor lamps, bracket lamps, candles, lanterns, and torches, should contain small incandescent lamps of very low wattage. Nothing is more annoying to an audience than to be forced to look at a bright source of light on the stage. Even a wax candle is frequently too bright. Obviously, any lighting instrument must be so masked that it is not visible from any seat in the house.

Around the backings of the set, illumination should be much less than on the acting area; in these locations short compartment striplights (see Chapter 4, p. 67) are adequate. They can be attached to the offstage side of the set itself. These striplights, moreover, are very useful on the floor to illuminate ground rows in situations where there is insufficient space for a 6-foot striplight with three circuits.

LIGHTING THE WALLS OF A SET

The actual walls of a set should have very little light on them, probably not more than from a twentieth to a twenty-fifth part of the light on the acting area. This keeps the emphasis and the attention of the audience on the actors instead of on the background. More fundamental than the matter of relative emphasis is the fatigue that follows looking at large areas of bright light. In fact, a good play could fail because the set was as bright as the acting area. An important reason why illuminating a play by means of borderlights and footlights alone is wrong is that the background receives the same amount of light as the actors receive. Since a setting that is high in brightness would probably reflect more light than the average make-up, it would appear brighter than the actors' faces. Sometimes, however, it is necessary to increase the amount of illumination on the wall of a set beyond an appropriate degree. For example, if actors play up against the wall, the specific illumination must be high enough for adequate visibility, and this will cause spottiness on the wall that will have to be smoothed out by increasing the general illumination. The practice of using Fresnel lenses in upstage area spotlights has helped smooth out this difficulty to a large extent. Even if this objectionable increase is necessary, the upper part of the set can be kept darker by directing the striplights down. Then very little illumination other than footlighting will fall on the upper portion of the set. Since this light should be dim, it will add a pleasing color tonality to the set without making it too light. In general, one should always regulate and distribute the light on the setting so that the intensity decreases gradually from the bottom to the top.

BACKGROUND LIGHTING

The last element to be considered in the setting is the background. For this discussion the principal background elements are sky cycloramas and drops, and the period revival drop painted for a particular production. A cyclorama is the most difficult element in the setting to light effectively, probably because stage space is nearly always so limited that instruments have to be placed too close to the surface of the cyclorama. This condition makes an even distribution very difficult to maintain.

While a cyclorama ordinarily extends from an offstage position near one side of the proscenium arch to a similar position on the other side of the stage, seldom must the whole of it be lighted at once. From one-half to two-thirds of the surface is as much as is commonly used for any one play. The size of the area has little to do with the difficulty or simplicity of the task of lighting a cyclorama. The difference is largely in the number of instruments necessary. The whole problem, then, is that of producing general illumination evenly distributed over a smooth surface. Of course, variations in quantity and color in this distribution are necessary. The base of the cyclorama, including an area extending about 10 or 12 feet up, can be lighted best by short striplights from 6 feet to 7 feet 6 inches long. Such instruments, with a maximum wattage in each lamp of 150 with the reflectors on 6-inch centers (see Chapter 4, pp. 64 and 65), are the right size for all cyclorama base lighting in common practice in an average theatre. Employing an instrument with reflectors on 6-inch centers, one should use 150-watt lamps, although there is much more blue needed than green or red. With such instruments color mixing can be fairly close to the instrument, so that an 18-inch ground row is high enough to mask the mixing, and the instrument can be placed within 5 feet of the cyclorama surface. For a better distribution of light, however, the instruments should be at least 6 or 7 feet from the surface. Larger instruments can be used where greater wattage is necessary, if space allows them to be placed at least 6 feet from the surface and if taller ground rows are used to mask them. This condition will obtain in large theatres only. The reader is no doubt familiar with the fact that these instruments produce the changes in color necessary for sunsets and sunrises. By the use of the primary colors in three circuits, subtle changes in quantity and color can be made at the control board to produce beautiful sunrises and sunsets of the cloudless variety. The short striplights are connected end to end in an arc-like formation in front of the cyclorama. As explained on p. 63 in Chapter 4, the striplight without the reflectors, using R40 lamps and 55° spread roundels, gives a better distribution than the other type when the striplights are forced too close to the surface.

The upper part of the cyclorama is lighted by floodlights mounted on a batten or frame, as explained in Chapter 4. To accomplish changes from daylight to night, or vice versa, it is necessary to have these in two circuits. If space is limited and the instruments have to be within 6 or 8 feet of the surface, they must be very close together in a row with every other instrument on the same circuit. A more nearly even distribution can be acquired, however, if the instruments are placed 15 or 20 feet from the surface and are mounted on two battens. Under these circumstances, like colors can be closer together. Floodlights of 500 watts are large enough for almost any cyclorama.

Again in the case of cycloramas, we find that the errors in lighting fall on the side of too much light rather than too little. The cyclorama needs no more than between a twenty-fifth and a fiftieth of the illumination on the acting area. In color the daylight sky can be produced with light blue color media (see Chapter 6). It should be neither toward the green nor toward the violet. A dark blue that transmits no red is hard to obtain in cheap color media, but for a night sky the medium must be neither green-blue nor purple. Only a strictly pure blue, so far as the eye is concerned, will carry the illusion of sky. One rarely sees a stage sky that is dim enough and of the proper hue.

While only sky cycloramas have been discussed above, any surface that partly encloses the acting area of the stage might, generally speaking, be called a cyclorama. In fact, a drapery of monk's cloth, velour, or any other material hung in folds might be considered in this general class. The method of lighting these is much the same as that described above, but much more variety in color is often used over the whole surface, depending on the purpose to which the drapery is put. Floodlights on stands are sometimes used as supplementary sources if the height of the material is not more than 12 or 14 feet and the width 20 feet or less. Flat surfaces of material hung from battens, called drops, are really substitutes for cycloramas. When a drop is used as a sky backing, the lighting is done according to the method described above or by means of a borderlight; striplight sections connected end to end serve the same purpose. On the other hand, in producing plays from the nineteenth century or earlier, painted drops, wings, and borders are often made a part of the setting if the play is done in the style of its original production. These drops and their companions, the wings and the borders, look best in dim general illumination produced with a border (striplights) placed parallel to the drop and about 6 or 8 feet from it. A row of floodlights is a satisfactory substitute, but spotlights cannot be used because shadows and an uneven distribution distort the painting. Even with borderlighting, however, shadows may appear if the actors are allowed to play very near the drop. Natural shadows produced by light are always incongruent with painted ones. When painted drops must be used, the only satisfactory light for them is general illumination that is as nearly shadowless as possible.

PRELIMINARY PLANS FOR PRODUCTION

If one is now familiar with the general approach, he is ready to begin planning the lighting in the production of a specific play. The obvious way to begin is with a good knowledge of the text. If one is planning or designing the lighting, he must read the script, first for its general emotional impact and mood, and then again for its detailed requirements that concern light. Before the next step, which is consulting with the director and designers of scenery and costumes, the lighting designer might ask himself several questions. What is the mood; what is the emotional effect of the play? What is the playwright trying to say? Is this a serious play, a comedy, a tragedy, or a melodrama? What is its style? Can these general matters be expressed in terms of quantity, color, and distribution of light? Should the light be evenly distributed, with subtle tints of color, such as one might use in many of Chekhov's plays? What are the time, place, and season in each scene? How is light to be motivated; that is, shall the light on the actor and the set seem to come from the sun or sky? Or should the light seem to come from artificial sources such as table and floor lamps, candles, or gas luminaires? And finally, which functions of light should be emphasized? These questions are a part of the lighting designer's thinking as he studies the play in detail and makes appropriate notes. Some of the answers will be found in the text. Others will come from the designer's imagination and analytical ability, or from consultations with the director and other designers. If the theatre staff consists of several people, the planning of a production becomes a cooperative matter led by the director. In a one-man organization he may have to answer all of these questions alone, but in the educational theatre we can assume that the production of a play is a learning process for students and that those with experience and imagination will have a part in the lighting plans under discussion.

After consultation with his fellow artists and an examination of the scene and costume sketches, the lighting designer is ready to make the detailed plans commonly called a *lighting layout,* or a *light plot.* The light plot includes a floor plan of the set, such as the one in Figure 9–4, a longitudinal section, an instrument schedule, and a control board cue sheet. The plan and section show the position of each instrument and the area lighted by that instrument. The instrument schedule, using the same symbols, shows the type, wattage, outlet, dimmer, color, and so forth for each instrument. While the section is not always necessary, it is helpful in indicating instrument heights above the floor and the vertical angles of the beams of light. Although the control board cue sheets must be prepared in part before the lighting rehearsals, the dimmer readings may be changed frequently before the final dress rehearsal.

Complete communication and proper coordination of the work of all of the artists concerned is highly essential to the success of any dramatic production. Lighting is sometimes easier to change than scenery and costumes. But it must light the actor even if holes have to be cut in the scenery to allow light to reach the acting area. Refocusing, changing a color filter, and even moving a lighting instrument during the dress rehearsal period are not too difficult. On the other hand, good mounting positions for the instruments at the proper angles to light the actor most effectively need consideration from the beginning. Careful early planning prevents last minute difficulties.

A SPECIFIC EXAMPLE

The first act of Jean Giraudoux's *Ondine* has been selected as a good example of lighting a combined exterior and interior scene. This play is based on an old German myth of the Middle Ages; in fact, there have been several plays and stories based on this legend. In the present version Giraudoux has given us a romantic treatment of the old tale that mixes fantasy and realism in a delightfully amusing French manner. Comedy, satire, and social comment are combined to dramatize in poetic prose the story of the ill-fated water sprite, Ondine, who wanted to be a human being and who fell in love with the simple knight errant, Ritter Hans. This is a beautiful romantic drama.

This play was the first production in the new theatre at California State University, San Diego, designed by Professor Don W. Powell, with direction and lighting by the writer. In this, as in planning the lighting of any play, one must begin by a careful study of the script to find its type (comedy, tragedy, or melodrama), its style (romanticism, realism, symbolism, expressionism, etc.), and its mood. Many readings of the script and conferences with the costume designer and scene designer led us to agree that we wanted to do a romantic fantasy with the occasional realistic touches required by the text. Its mood changes from the romantic and humorous in the beginning (with a few serious warnings) to death and grief at the end.

Returning to Chapter 1, we must apply the principles and analysis of light established there to the planning of the lighting in Act I of *Ondine*. The setting of Act I, which Professor Powell created, is a fisherman's cottage hanging over the edge of a magic lake. As one can see in Figure 9–3, the form of the cottage is romantic in line and is raised several feet above the stage floor to suggest hanging in space when the fog rolled under as well as around the cottage. Some of the "sister" ondines made their entrances from under the cottage. Since the designer used no ceiling, he created a sense of space around the small cottage, allowing the lighting designer to achieve a greater variety in angles for his spotlight beams.

First he had to consider the two kinds of light, general and specific. In this play general illumination would have flattened the whole appearance, killing the effect of the cottage hanging over the lake. In fact, Fresnel spotlights would have produced too much spill light and diffusion, so sharply focused ellipsoidal spotlights were used exclusively in this set. In quantity the light was medium bright in the more romantic and realistic part of the act and considerably dimmer in the transformation scene where Hans is tempted by the ondine "sisters." In color the light was warm (pink) until changed to the medium blue of the transformation. In distribution, the light was made fairly smooth by overlapping area instruments before the transformation. After it, the areas were spotty, with almost no light between the special areas where Hans and the ondine "sisters" worked. Thus the three controllable properties combined to effect the transformation from romanticism and realism to fantasy.

The functions played their part in the following manner. In this example the first function, selective visibility, is particularly important. In any production, as mentioned in Chapter 1, visibility is our first concern. In many "atmospheric" scenes visibility is sacrificed; this is wrong because the members of the audience demand that they see the actors' faces, especially near the beginning of a play when people are getting acquainted with the characters. Here, this applies particularly to Ondine, Hans, and Ondine's foster parents. Complete visibility is not as essential for the "sister" ondines. The selective aspect of this function is accomplished by the narrow beams of the ellipsoidal spotlights carefully focused to small areas with almost no spill to other areas. Before the transformation, the area light was selectively confined to the interior of the cottage with no illumination on the rock and forestage. Of course, there was medium blue general illumination and the cloud projection on the cyclorama. After the transformation, while the "sister" ondines were tempting Hans, the control board operators cross-faded to dim blue areas within the cottage and dimmed up on Hans in individual areas as he moved from place to place in the cottage and also on individual "sister" ondines on the rocks and across the forestage. Several of the ondines performed individually with Hans, and the areas were dimmed up individually as the dialogue continued between Hans and various ondines. All of this, of course, was selective visibility.

The second function, revelation of form, was being accomplished by the very fact that spotlights (specific illumination) were the only sources of light, producing highlights, shade, and shadow that added roundness, that is, a three-dimensional quality to actors and scenery. By keeping almost all of the area light away from the scenery, allowing essentially the floor reflections to light the scenery, a good contrast between actor and background obtained. This contributed to the vital, solid appearance of both the scenery and actors. As mentioned above, one can reinforce the separation of actor and background and reinforce the form-revealing function with back lighting. It is accomplished by a row of spotlights above and upstage of the actor at an angle of approximately 60°. The effect is of lighting the figure of the actor with highlights on the shoulders and in the hair. In the production of *Ondine* this was not possible because the teaser was so high that such instruments would have been visible to the first few rows of seats.

The third function, the illusion of nature, was not as important as it would be in a strictly realistic play, but it did play some part at times. In this Act I the sky was semirealistic in color and distribution of light, but the blue color tended to be romantic and possibly might have suggested night rather than the daytime indicated at the opening of the play. The clouds, as mentioned elsewhere, moved across the sky (cyclorama) but instead of being naturalistic were simplified or stylized in keeping with a more romantic approach. In the third act (not discussed here), which was an exterior, there was a semirealistic but essentially symbolic sunset changing into twilight. These effects accompanied the death of Hans and the return of Ondine to the world of the water.

The fourth function of light for the stage, composition, calls upon the lighting designer for a full understanding of composition from both the director's and the artist's points of view. Light must focus the attention of the audience as the direcor's focus with actors moves from place to place. As the actor turns from left to right (or vice versa), when one is working with two spotlights to an area from considerably different angles, one spotlight can be thought of as a key light and the other as a fill. When the turn takes place the control operator might dim down the key and dim up the fill, reversing the emphasis and exchanging key and fill. It is assumed that both instruments are spotlights. Such a change was made when Hans moved from one ondine down right to another one down left. This is one type of compositional change during the latter part of Act I.

The fifth function is mood. As stated in Chapter 1, this is the least tangible function and the most difficult to explain or discuss. To repeat, *Ondine* is a poetic and romantic play, and one senses the importance of projecting its mood even in a superficial reading. With more careful reading the variety in moods is certainly evident. In production the rhythm of the lines, the actors' movements, the background music, costumes, scenery, and lighting—all must be integrated into one mood at any one moment in the production. But

Figure 9-3 Giraudoux's *Ondine*, design by Don W. Powell, lighting and directing by H. D. Sellman, California State University Theatre, San Diego. Notice lens projected (moving) clouds.

Figure 9–5 Jean Genet's *The Maids*, at California State Theatre, San Diego, designed by Don W. Powell, lighting by Merrill Lessley, direction by Mack Owen.

there were various moods as the play progressed. In Act I the establishing mood of the supernatural, the mood of romance, and a threatening mood of uncertainty as Ondine makes her pact with the Old One are present, and many questions involving mood are raised with the closing of Act I. Specifically, the mood was accomplished or suggested with light first by brightness or relatively dim light, by light in the cottage surrounded by comparative darkness, and by dim light combined with the carbon dioxide fog in the temptation scene with the "sister" ondines. The changing of the light on these ondines from silhouette to a single shaft also adds to the mood of mystery and suspense. Color, too, is always a factor in mood. The cottage set was a shaded neutral gray spattered with pink, blue, and lavender tints so that it would reflect both ends of the spectrum. The costumes also lent themselves to the change from warm to cool. Hans wore his knight errant off-white with silver armor and Ondine's first costume was a filmy combination of grays. These two costumes looked well in the pink and lavender light of the earlier scenes and equally well in the blue light toward the end of the act. Ondine's parents wore simple peasants' warm earth colors suited to their characters and to the warm light in which they appeared. Thus the pink and lavender area light within the cottage expressed warmth and romance within, while the blue sky (cyclorama) gave us the mystery of the enchanted lake and forest outside. During the temptation of Hans the change to blue areas for the "sister" ondines and on Hans inside the cottage brought the mystery, enchantment, and threat closer to us. In such a way light can contribute its mood to the mood of the whole production.

THE LIGHT PLOT

After the lighting designer has made a careful analysis and examination of the text of the play and discussed it with his fellow artists, he is ready for a study of the scene designer's sketch and his ground plan. This ground plan will be the graphic basis of the light plot shown in Figure 9–4. Although not shown here, there is sometimes a longitudinal section showing the teaser height (the height of the cottage above the floor in this set), the vertical angles of the light beams, and the mounting height of the bridge and other batten-mounted lighting instruments. Always there must be an instrument schedule and some type of control board cue sheet containing the dimmer readings. If there are many cue changes with new readings of many dimmers, each set of readings should be on a separate sheet.

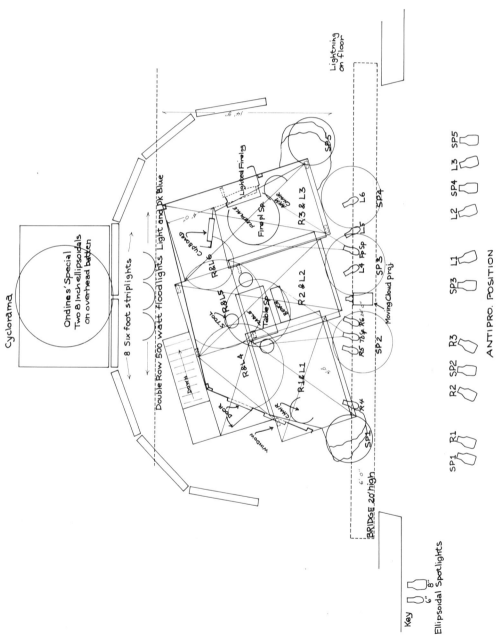

Figure 9–4 Light plot for *Ondine*, Act I.

Background Lighting

The cyclorama was lighted by eight 6-foot three-color striplights on the stage floor about 6 or 7 feet from the cyclorama surface. A ground row (not shown in Figure 9–4) concealed these striplights. The upper part of the cyclorama was lighted by 28 500-watt floodlights, half with light-blue media and half with dark-blue media, mounted on a double-row frame attached to one of the regular stage battens about 14 feet from the cyclorama and about 35 above the stage floor. To complete the background (sky) lighting, a moving cloud effect was added to the cyclorama by means of a lens projector. The projector included a 5000-watt lamp, the usual reflector and condensing system, and an objective lens of 4½-inch focal length (see Chapter 5). The cloud effect itself was a positive film strip, 12 feet long, that rolled horizontally by means of a very slow-speed back-geared motor. The projector is shown in the middle of the light bridge in Figure 9–4, where it projected the clouds over the wall of the cottage to the cyclorama.

Acting Area Lighting

Since the cottage was a relatively small room, 22 feet wide by 12 feet deep, it was divided into six lighting areas instead of at least eight that are needed in this theatre for a set occupying the full proscenium opening. The three upstage areas in the cottage were lighted by six 750-watt 6-inch lens ellipsoidal spotlights mounted on the bridge. These areas are shown in Figure 9–4 as circles marked R & L4, R & L5, and R & L6. The corresponding instruments marked L4, L5, and L6 and R4, R5, and R6 are shown on the bridge. The three downstage areas shown as rectangles and marked R & L1, R & L2, and R & L3 were lighted by six 8-inch lens ellipsoidal spotlights each with 1000-watt lamps, mounted on a batten in the antiproscenium position. They are shown in Figure 9–4 as R1, R2, and R3 and L1, L2, and L3. In addition to the conventional six areas and 12 spotlights, it was necessary to have a table special and a fireplace special of 750 watts (6-inch lens ellipsoidals) mounted on the bridge that allowed these two special areas to remain brighter when the regular area were dimmed for the fantasy transformation.

When the "sister" ondines arose from the lake at the rear, the six warm areas cross-faded to six cool areas (medium blue) not shown in the light plot of Figure 9–4 but covering the same areas. Twelve of these 750-watt 6-inch lens ellipsoidals were mounted on an upper batten of the bridge, producing beams of a slightly higher angle than on the warm areas. These instruments and two 1000-watt 8-inch ellipsoidals on a batten directly over the middle of the cottage were omitted to prevent cluttering and to clarify the light plot for a beginning student. The "sister" ondines arose from the rocks on the rectangular hydraulic lift shown upstage of the set. The circle lighted by the 8-inch specials is shown within the rectangle. During the transformation, when the interior of the cottage was dim, the two specials came up on the ondines posed on the rocks behind the cottage. They were seen through the back wall of the cottage covered with scrim that was nearly transparent when there was little or no light on the front side of it. When the light was at its maximum level, the ondines moved from the rocks and danced their way through the fog to the five special areas in front and at the corners of the cottage. The special instruments for these areas (Sp. 1 through Sp. 5) were 8-inch 1000-watt ellipsoidals mounted on the same anteproscenium batten (in port over audience) with the other downstage area instruments. The "sister" ondines disappeared with a reverse cross-fade back to warm light in the cottage for the final love scene between Hans and Ondine. There were two lightning cues near the beginning of the play. They were accomplished by a 60-ampere double-carbon remotely controlled arc instrument placed on the floor just out of sight lines on stage left. It produced open-arc lightning flashes on the cyclorama.

Following the ground-plan light plot (and section if needed), the lighting designer or an assistant made an instrument list or schedule that stated the number, type, designation, color, stage outlet, where it is to be plugged and mounted, dimmer, and so forth. A typical one might look something like this.

Type	Mfgr.	Lens	Wattage	Position	Outlet	Dimmer	Color	Location
Ellips.	Century	6-inch	750	R6	Br 10	28	Pink	Bridge
Stplgt	Kliegl		600 each	Flr	Fl L8	58	BGR	Floor
Ellips.	Century	8-inch	1000	R1	Be 6	42	Lav.	Antepro 1

Of course, this would continue until every instrument was accounted for. Since it is a waste of time to dismount every bridge and anteproscenium instrument after every play, some of these may need only be shifted on the batten and connected to a nearby outlet. The bridge (or first pipe) was brought to the floor and additional instruments selected and brought from storage. Other needed battens were brought down for floodlights and perhaps additional spotlights as mentioned above for *Ondine*. When the clamps were tightened and the bridge and batten moved back to their "trim" position (for sight lines, correct angle of beam, etc.), the instruments were rough focused. Checks were made to see that all ellipsoidal framing shutters were open before the light came on. Shutters are more easily burned and distorted if they are closed with the light on. Furthermore, the temperature within will rise and possibly damage the reflector and shorten the life of the lamp. Final accurate focusing cannot be done ordinarily until the set is in place. Many times a framing shutter must be adjusted to line up with a wall of a set or the frame around a doorway. If a framing shutter is making an unwanted line on a piece of scenery, the line can be softened by defocusing the lens until the image of the shutter opening is no longer sharp. As suggested, these adjustments in the *Ondine* production were made after the first set was in place. The fire log effect was placed and adjusted and finally, the horizon (cyclorama) striplights were rolled in and arranged as shown on the light plot. Then the color frames were added to spotlights and floodlights.

Only Act I of *Ondine* has been discussed in detail, but there are certain problems in coordination with the other two acts that need to be clarified. The Act I set was rolled on and off. Before it could be shifted off, the fire log had to be disconnected and the three horizon striplights on the stage right side had to be rolled farther upstage for clearance and the setting for Act II set-up. Fortunately, there were a sufficient number of spotlights so that an entirely new group were focused for Acts II and III. The only problem was to integrate the instruments on the bridge and in the anteproscenium position. When one has only a minimum number of instruments, refocusing the area spotlights and changing the color frames between scenes is a difficult task when time is short. If a theatre has a bridge, several operators can remain there, and chalk markings on the instruments may help in refocusing. Furthermore, a floor supervisor may be needed to aid in precise adjustments.

When the set-up described above was complete, and all of the instruments were connected through the interconnecting (patch) panel, the lighting designer was ready for a lighting rehearsal without the cast. The stage manager was on hand to walk about and show the light crew where the actors would be at specific cues. A few adjustments in focus are always necessary when relating the light to the actor for the first time.

The three control operators had already arranged the dimmers in convenient groups and had marked a script with warnings and exact cues. After the curtain went up, the grand master dimmer was raised from black to the specified reading, followed by the first scene master, which controlled the warm area light. When this master reached its readings, the first line of the play was spoken. There were music cues, then thunder several times accompanied by lightning (operated by a single switch, not a dimmer control). The next light cue was at the transformation. On that cue the warm area scene master was dimmed while a group master controlling the spotlights upstage on the "sister" ondines was raised. They were seen through the set as the cool (blue) scene master was dimmed up to a low reading. As explained above and diagrammed on the light plot, this scene master included the cottage at a dim reading, the rocks at the downstage ends, and the specials in front of the cottage. As these ondines came downstage, the control operators raised the lighting level on individual ondines as each tempted Hans. He, too, was given more light in specific areas. When the temptation scene was over, the transformation was cross-faded to the earlier warm distribution of light, with more emphasis on the specials and certain areas during the love scene. The control operators made these last changes with individual dimmers rather than with scene or group masters. The act ended with a slow fade to black by means of the grand master. Figure 9–3 is of some assistance in visualizing the procedure. During the lighting rehearsal, the control operators rehearsed these changes a number of times and made adjustments of dimmer readings until the lighting designer and director were satisfied that the control operators were ready for the three dress rehearsals. Usually, by the end of the third dress rehearsal they are ready for opening night. This outline of the steps that one follows from the study and analysis of a play through to the dress rehearsals and opening night should give the student some idea of this writer's practice in lighting a play.

SECOND EXAMPLE

The second example is from Jean Genet's *The Maids,* a long one-act play produced in the Drama Department at San Diego State College. The interior set shown in Figure 9–5 was designed by Professor Don W. Powell and lighted by Dr. Merrill Lessley. According to Dr. Lessley, *The Maids* is reminiscent of Pirandello's *Six Characters in Search of an Author* and his *Henry the IV.* These plays demonstrate how easily "fantasy becomes truth and truth fantasy." Dr. Lessley, in analyzing *The Maids,* found certain circular actions in which two opposite forms enter and exit in such a way that it is difficult to distinguish one from the other. Here, as in Pirandello's plays, we have "appearance versus reality." If one studies *The Maids* carefully, he will notice that the play is a sort of ritual in which the maids, Solange and Claire, become different characters whenever

Madame, the head of the household, is not present. When Madame is on stage, both Solange and Claire drop their masks and revert to their true characters as maids. When Madame leaves they resume their ritual of false identities. As the lighting designer, Dr. Lessley tried to create an environment in which he set the mood for both actors and spectators. Through highlight, shadow, and color he suggested Genet's circular movement, in which "reality and unreal appearance dissolve into and emerge out of each other." He accomplished the five functions of stage lighting in a fairly conventional way when Madame was on stage. There was a better balance in area lighting and the setting was given a simpler flatter appearance, a more realistic sense of dimension. When the maids were alone, however, a gradual change of mood took place by brightening the pink area instruments and dimming the blue ones. This change produced greater contrast in the area lighting and lengthened the shadows. Furthermore, under these circumstances, the set itself assumed a new appearance through a change in light. By changing the direction of light on the set to an almost vertical angle, the three-dimensional detail on the walls of the set (see Figure 9–5) stood out in a dream-like, unreal, almost macabre manner. Different highlights and long shadows were primarily responsible for this strong emphasis on the fifth function, mood—a very different mood created by light alone.

The order of procedure in this case was very similar to that in our first example. After carefully studying and analyzing the play as described above, the designer consulted the director and scene designer to exchange ideas. Then he prepared the light plot in Figure 9–6 using the scene designer's ground plan. As one can see, the set is a rather shallow one, with the downstage areas as much on the forestage as they are above the curtain line. These conditions led to the decision to light both up- and downstage areas from the first anteproscenium position. The bridge and three overhead battens were used for special instruments. Because of the width and shape of the floor area within the set, the downstage space was divided into four areas and the upstage space into three areas. About 20 8-inch ellipsoidal spotlights remained in the first anteproscenium position; so no mounting was necessary, just shifting along the pipe and selecting the proper positions for the 14 instruments needed for this production (1 through 14 in Figure 9–6). Since the downstage areas were a somewhat shorter distance away than the upstage ones, the eight spotlights illuminating areas 1 through 4 contained 750-watt lamps and those covering areas 5, 6, and 7 were provided with 1000-watt lamps.

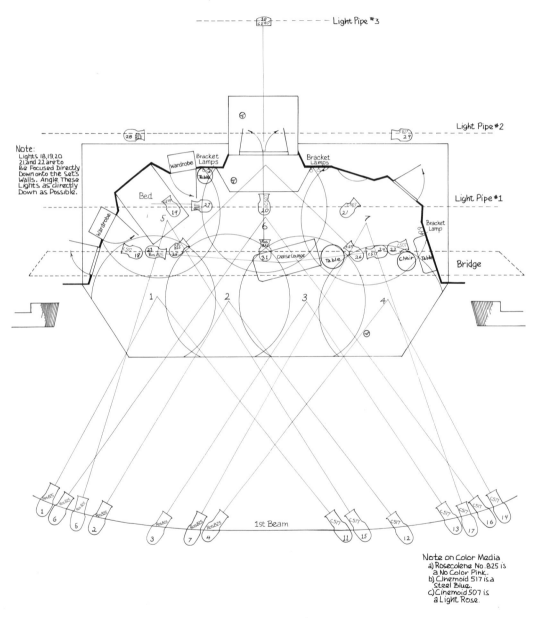

Figure 9–6 Light plot for *The Maids*. California State Theatre, 1970. Set design by Don W. Powell. Light design by Merrill J. Lessley.

The bridge too was well provided with 500-watt six-inch lens ellipsoidals; so adjusting and focusing these specials was easily accomplished. Spotlight 31 is an example in which a special was required to be framed on the doorway at center, a common practice where area spotlights focused this high would spill on the set too much.

To make the change to the "unreal" condition, a batten just above the set was selected (no ceiling was used), Light Pipe 1, where four 500-watt 6-inch ellipsoidal spotlights were mounted and focused from a tall ladder to produce beams of light almost straight down on the set as mentioned above and shown in Figure 9–6. On Light Pipe 2 two more 500-watt 6-inch lens ellipsoidal spotlights added supplemental sidelighting for actors standing upstage of the center door. Their front lighting was from instrument 31 on the bridge. The final mounting and focusing chore was a 14-inch parallel beam projector with a 1500-watt lamp on Light Pipe 3. This produced moonlight through the center door. Just before each instrument was focused, it was plugged into a nearby outlet and another light crew member connected it to a dimmer of appropriate capacity at the interconnecting panel. Then color frames were added as shown on the light plot, with a number and notes explaining the meaning of each number. No cyclorama or background lighting was needed because the set was surrounded by black draperies. Just as in our first example, an instrument schedule was prepared showing all pertinent information before the work of mounting, plugging, and focusing took place.

Again, when the focusing and adjusting were finished, the lighting designer worked with his control console operators. They read and marked their script and studied the cue problems and gradual changes in the transitions discussed and described above. Their control console had five scenes (five presets); so the opening curtain readings were set up on the first scene. When Madame entered they made a smooth change to the "reality" readings on Scene 2 by dimming down or cross-fading on the Scene 1 master to the Scene 2 master. On this particular console (Figure 8–12) such a change can be made with two hands, and the two scene masters on it can be handled with one movement on a single scene fader. These changes were continued with fading transitions from Scene 2 to Scene 3, Scene 3 to Scene 4, and then from Scene 4 to Scene 5 as the play progressed. This lighting design was fairly simple, with only four changes. In plays with many scenes and cues, the console operators are resetting the first four scenes while Scene 5 is in progress, and this may go on and on.

Figure 9–7   Design for New York production of *Avanti,* design and lighting by Donald Oenslager.

It is to be hoped that these two fairly simple examples of planning lighting for plays will give the student an idea of well-organized procedures, and by following their general plan will lead him to the first lighting rehearsal, at least three smooth dress rehearsals, and perfect handling of the lighting control problems in performances. Not everyone is a calm, intelligent control operator at the first dress rehearsal of his first production. Actors rehearse 30 or more times and still are forgiven for imperfect dress rehearsals and even performances. Console operators are expected to be perfect at the first dress rehearsal. Very few of us are more than human.

To provide an example of the lighting of a professional Broadway production, Donald Oenslager has kindly allowed me to use his design and light plot[3] for *Avanti,* produced by Morris Jacobs and Jerry Whyte. The electrical equipment schedule and switchboard layout are also included for clarification. The reader will notice that all of the instruments are numbered and their location is shown, but contrary to educational theatre practice, the lighted areas are not indicated (see Figures 9–7 and 9–8).

Through the courtesy of the late Jean Rosenthal and her secretary, Miss Eleanor Denny, I am including another Broadway theatre light plot. This one is for a musical, based on the stage play *The*

[3] Assisted by Klaus Holm.

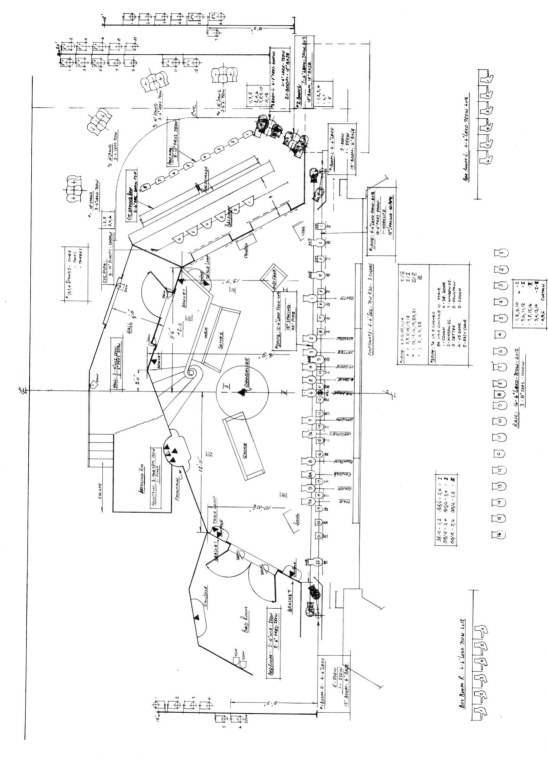

Figure 9–8 Light plot for *Avanti*. Design and lighting by Donald Oenslager.

Electrical Equipment Schedule For Avanti

Producers:	Morris Jacobs	Electrician: Bobby Siegel
	Jerry Whyte	LOAD OUT JAN. 5, 1968,
Designer:	Donald Oenslager	New Haven, Conn.

Rail	16 6″ Lekos—750-W—6×12 lens	4 4-way
	8 Asbestos-wrapped cables—8 2-way branch-offs pans, hangers, etc.	
Box Boom Right	6 6″ Lekos—750-W—6×12 lens—sidearms	3 4-way
	3 Asbestos-wrapped cables—3 2-way branch-offs	
	6 6″ High hats—1 20′ boom, 18″ base	
Box Boom Left	6 6″ Lekos—750-W—6×12 lens—sidearms	see BB/R
	3 Asbestos-wrapped cables—3 2-way branch-offs	
	6 6″ High hats—1 20′ boom, 18″ base	
Foots	4 6′ Sections—750-WR30 low units	2 4-way
No. 1 Pipe	4 6″ Lekos—50-W—6×12 lens	4 6-way
	18 6″ Fresnels—500-W	
	1 Worklight	
	26 Cables	
	1 40′ pipe, stiffeners, asbestos	
No. 2 Pipe	12 6″ Lekos—500-W—6×9 lens	12 aux
	14 Cables	see No. 1 pipe
	1 40′ pipe, stiffeners	
No. 1 Boom Right	6 6″ Lekos—6×9 lens: 5 500-W, 1 250-W—3 9″ sidearms; 3 24″ sidearms	1 6-way
	5 Cables, 4 2-way branch-offs	3 aux
	1 15′ boom, 6″ flange, C-clamp safety at base, asbestos	
No. 1 Boom Left	6 6″ Lekos—6×9 lens: 5 500-W, 1 250-W—3 9″ sidearms; 3 24″ sidearms	3 aux
	5 Cables, 4 2-way branch-offs	
	1 15′ boom, 6″ flange, C-clamp safety at base, asbestos	
Bedroom	2 6″ Fresnels—250-W—flange and sidearm	1 aux
	2 10″ Wizards—250-W—flange and sidearm	1 aux
	2 Cables, 2 2-way branch-offs	
Hall	2 6″ Fresnels—500-W—flange and sidearm	2 aux
	2 10″ Wizards—250-W—flange and sidearm	1 aux
	3 Cables, 1 2-way branch off	
Brackets, etc.	U.S.C. Brackets 1 cable	
	D.S.R. Brackets 1 cable	
	Chandelier 1 cable	
	Table lamp 1 cable	
	Fountain 2 cables	

Cyc. Pipe	6 16″ Scoops—1000-W—C-clamps— color frames 6 Cables 14′ pipe, stiffeners	2 4-way
Proj. Pipe	8 10″ Beam projectors—750-W—C-clamps 4 Cables, 4 2-way branch-offs 12′ pipe, stiffeners	2 4-way
Ground Row	2 6′ Sections—300-W—3-color 3 Cables	3 4-way
No. 2 Boom *Left*	7 6″ Lekos: 1 750-W, 6×12 lens; 4 750-W, 6×9 lens; 2 500-W, 6×9 lens—sidearms 6 Cables, 5 2-way branch-offs 1 18′ boom, 18″ base	1 6-way 1 4-way
No. 3 Boom *Left*	6 8″ Fresnels—1000-W—sidearms 6 6″ Lekos: 1 750-W, 6×12 lens; 4 750-W, 6×9 lens; 1 500-W, 6×9 lens—sidearms 10 Cables, 3 2-way branch-offs 1 20′ boom, 18″ base 6 8″ Barndoors	2 4-way see No. 2 BL 1 4-way
Stands	12 6″ Lekos—750-W—6×9 lens—sidearms 6 Cables, 3 2-way branch-offs and extensions 4 10′ stands, 18″ base	3 4-way
Boards	3 3000/1500-W—14 plate 2 500-W—12 plate aux.	
Misc.	4 3″ Fresnels—100-W 2 Cables, 2 2-way branch-offs 6″ High hats 6″ Barndoors 5-way switchbox (for practicals) 5 Cables	

Switch Board Layout For Avanti

1. Rail—1, 2, 9, 10—I
2. Rail—5, 6, 11, 12—II
3. Rail—7, 8, 15, 16—III
4. Rail—3, 4, 13, 14—I–III
5. Foots—Warm
6. Foots—Cool
7. No. 1 Pipe—1, 3, 6, 10, 11, 14—I/IV
8. No. 1 Pipe—5, 7, 8, 15, 17, 18—II/V
9. No. 1 Pipe—12, 13, 16, 19, 20, 21—
   III/VI
10. No. 1 Pipe—2, 4, 9, 22—VII
11. No. 1 Boom R/L—1, 2, 3
12. Aux. 47–52
13. Aux. 29–34
14. Aux. 35–40

12/47. No. 1 Boom L.—4
48. No. 1 Boom L.—5
49. No. 1 Pipe—1A
50. No. 1 Boom R.—4
51. No. 1 Pipe—23—stair
52. No. 1 Pipe—24—stair
13/29. No. 2 Pipe—1—couch
30. No. 2 Pipe—9—couch
31. No. 2 Pipe—2—window DS
32. No. 2 Pipe—7—window US
33. No. 2 Pipe—3—settee
34. No. 2 Pipe—5—easy chair

15. Aux. 41–46
16. Cyc. Pipe—1, 3, 5—dark blue
17. Cyc. Pipe—2, 4, 6—light blue
18. Propector Pipe—1, 3, 5, 7—Moon
19. Propector Pipe—2, 4, 6, 8—Sun
20. Ground Row—light blue
21. Ground Row/No. 2 Boom L.—
        5—amber
22. No. 3 Boom L.—1, 3, 5—Moon
23. No. 3 Boom L.—7, 8, 9, 10—
        sun in window
24. No. 3 Boom L.—2, 4, 6—sun
25. No. 2 Boom L.—6, 7/ No. 3 Boom
        L.—11, 12—late sun
26. Cyc. Back Light—windows
27. Cyc. Back Light—light blue
28. Cyc. Back Light—late sun

53. Rail—ABC curtain
54. Box Boom R/L—1, 2/5, 6—I
55. Box Boom R/L—3, 4/3, 4—II
56. Box Boom R/L—5, 6/1, 2—III
57. No. 2 Boom L.—1, 2, 3, 4—moon
58. Ground Row—N.C.
59. No. 4 Boom L.—1, 2, 3, 4—sun

Misc.—lamps, fountain

14/35. No. 2 Pipe—4—US door
36. No. 2 Pipe—6—SR door
37. No. 2 Pipe—8—fountain
38. No. 2 Pipe—7A—USR corner
39. No. 2 Pipe—8A—USR console
40. No. 2 Pipe—10—stair

15/41. Hall—Fresnel
42. Hall—Wizard
43. Bedroom—Fresnel
44. Bedroom—Wizard
45. Chandelier
46. Brackets

Fourposter, called *I Do, I Do,* designed by Oliver Smith (Figure 9–9). It is a one-set production with the light plot shown in Figure 9–10 and the hanging plan shown in Figure 9–11. For simplicity I have omitted the third sheet showing the elevations of the side lighting and the location of the instruments on the balcony front. As in the previous light plot of a Broadway production by Donald Oenslager for *Avanti,* emphasis is on the precise location of each lighting instrument, primarily on battens.

In the former case the lighting was done by the designer himself,[4] in the latter by a well-known lighting designer who has lighted many New York productions in which the scene designs were done by others. Both procedures are common in the commercial theatre as well as in the educational theatre.

LIGHT AND OTHER STAGING PRACTICES

The imaginative changes in theatre architecture in recent years are a distinct challenge to the lighting designer. Of course, some will say

[4] With the assistance of Klaus Holm.

Figure 9–9   The single set for *I Do, I Do,* design by Oliver Smith, lighting by Jean Rosenthal. (Photo Courtesy Friedman-Abeles.)

that the arena, theatre-in-the-round, thrust stage, and other variants from the conventional proscenium theatre are not new but revivals of theatre forms that have been in and out of style ever since the outdoor theatre of the ancient Greeks. In such theatres our problem as lighting designers is first to consult with architects who are designing new theatres and renovating and modifying older buildings so that our lighting problems are simplified and that some thought about the lighting of the actor and his background is integrated with the building structure. So often the ports, mounting arrangements, and concealed openings for lighting instruments are ignored or forgotten. Access for those who must mount and adjust them is equally neglected.

Some of these so-called thrust stages (the Guthrie Theatre in Minneapolis may be a good example) have been designed and constructed with the philosophy of deemphasizing scenery and of bringing the actor into closer relationship with the audience. Spectacle is

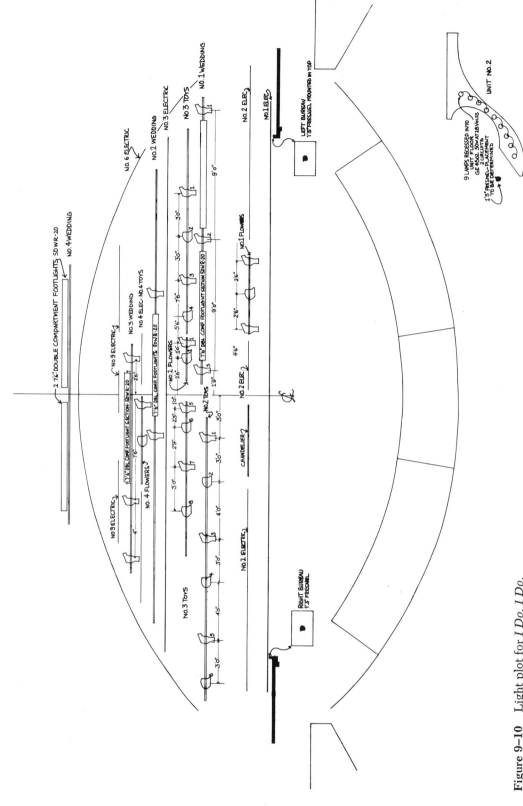

Figure 9–10 Light plot for *I Do, I Do.*

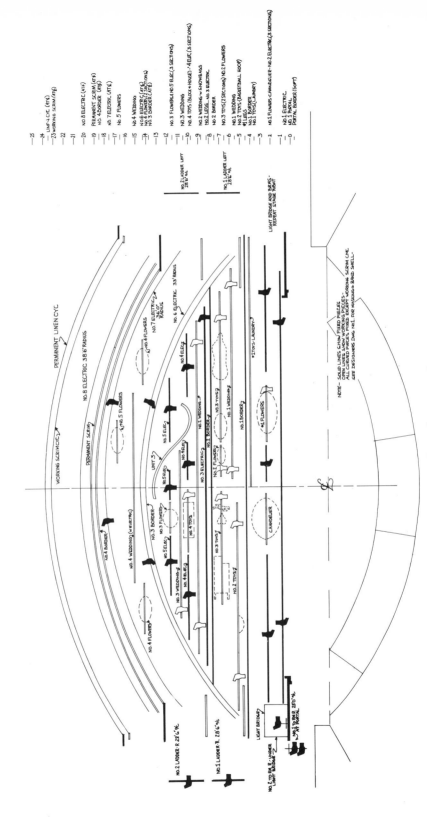

Figure 9–11 Hanging plan for *I Do, I Do*. Set design by Oliver Smith. Lighting by Jean Rosenthal.

Figure 9–12   The use of scrim for an entire set (Clifford Odets' *Awake and Sing*, Indiana University Theatre, 1965–1966) allows the director, with the careful assistance of the lighting designer, to portray foreground action alone, as shown in the large illustration, and also to align the action with the background. Direction by David Wiley, set design by George Bogusch, lighting design by Gary W. Gaiser.

frequently reduced to the effects of costume and movement and the functions of light are usually emphasized to the following degree: (1) Visibility is important (sometimes selective). (2) Revelation of form is by ellipsoidal spotlighting only. (3) Illusion of nature is greatly reduced. (4) Composition can vary from almost nothing to area lighting in front of projected forms, either in front or rear projected, or space patterns composed of shafts and pools of light. In the case of mood (5), the writer does not see much difference in light contributing to mood in this type of staging from that in proscenium staging. The loss of the opportunity to use the softening mood and effect of general illumination might limit one to a small degree, but the softer shadows of Fresnel lens spotlights, if their beams were directed toward the rear wall away from the audience, would probably suffice. The vertical and horizontal angles of the harsher light from ellipsoidal spotlights will affect mood through the variety of shadows produced by different angles. Of course color, as mentioned above, in using cool (blues and blue-greens) light for one mood and warm (lavender, pink, and orange) light for another, will make a strong contribution in this as well as in any type of staging.

If the audience is on three sides of the actor, and it usually is in this thrust type of stage, then the areas will have to be lighted from three sides. This means that each area lighted will need at least three and probably four ellipsoidal spotlights. Care must be taken to keep the glare and spill light from one side out of the spectators' eyes on the other. This involves a higher beam angle, causing deeper and longer shadows in actors' faces. Perhaps the two front lighting instruments could project their beams at a lower, more nearly desirable angle of 45 to 50°. In the larger thrust-stage theatres with a balcony, the ceilings and consequently the lighting ports are high and considerably distant from the stage. The longer throws resulting from that situation produce beams of light that include more spill and diffusion, the final effect being more like dull general illumination. Instruments selected for the long throws common in large thrust-stage theatres, as stated elsewhere, should be from the larger-diameter, higher-wattage variety. These narrower beamed instruments will operate at higher efficiency than others because the shutters can be left wide open or nearly so.

During the last half-century the arena theatre (in-the-round or central staging) has become increasingly popular, especially as a "second" theatre among college and university theatre departments. Many community theatres, as well as an occasional commercial theatre, have taken this general form. Generally, these stages have varied greatly in area, with shapes from square to circular to rectangular and even elliptical.

Since the lighting designer's problems and techniques will vary greatly with the form of the specific theatre, a somewhat different approach will be in order with each stage shape, ceiling height, and rise of one row of seats above another. For example, the ceiling height should be from 15 to 18 feet, the higher the better when lighting an actor near the front row from a spotlight mounted on the ceiling from the opposite side. The spectators in the front row frequently have light in their laps and are lucky if there isn't spill light in their eyes from spotlights opposite them. The spotlights should be mounted on or as near the ceiling as possible, with electrical outlets recessed in the ceiling. Without such outlets there will be a great deal of miscellaneous cable running about near the ceiling, with some of it undoubtedly drooping in an untidy manner. If the spotlights cannot be mounted directly to the ceiling it is common to use pipe frames, since nearly all spotlights are provided with pipe clamps. A frequently used instrument for the arena theatre is the 500-watt 6-inch Fresnel spotlight. Even with a funnel (high hat) it produces a soft edge beam that aggravates the spill and glare problem for the front-row audience. The writer prefers the 500-watt 6-inch plano-lens ellipsoidal spotlight or the 400- to 650-watt 3½-inch plano-lens spotlight (also ellipsoidal) as a second choice. The latter two contribute much less spill light, and the 6-inch ellipsoidal has the highest efficiency of the three.

Since there is ordinarily no background lighting, one can concentrate on the problems of area lighting. Each arena stage, with its specific size and shape, has its own lighting challenge. The whole acting area might be divided into a number of individually lighted areas by determining the spread of the most desirable spotlight for this specific ceiling height. An individual arena area requires four instruments, one from each direction for a rectangular area. Some designers use three instruments to an area on a circular stage. If the rectangular stage resolves itself into six areas, one often adds a seventh area in the very center, or simply adds specials to the basic 24 instruments for a special effect such as one or two actors left in brighter light while the six areas are dimmed.

Returning to the functions of light in the arena, the greatest emphasis is, of course, on visibility, with an occasional need for selectivity. The other function frequently emphasized is mood. As in other forms of staging, bright light is right for comedy and its related moods, and dimmer distributions are needed for more serious situations. Color is always important, but it must be in the color frames that cannot be changed conveniently between scenes in the usual arena theatre. As mentioned above, the common warm tints are pink, orange, and lavender and the cool ones, blue and blue-green. More saturated colors, although distorting to costumes and make-up, are sometimes appropriate for special effects. There is a certain monotony about arena staging that taxes the ingenuity of both the director and the lighting designer.

CURRENT TRENDS

Contemporary material written for the stage (some of it may be drama) frequently leans heavily on production facilities, especially stage lighting. It is quite likely that the poorer the material the greater the demand for effects. Especially in night clubs there is a trend toward entertainment with abstract moving color patterns reminiscent of Thomas Wilfred's Clavilux. The current ones are much more garish and intermixed with stroboscopic light and other electronically energized color variations. These effects are not necessarily poor, but they can stimulate and entertain only in small doses.

In both revivals of older plays and in new material there is a tendency to use projected spectacle that can be either still or moving. In a recent revival of *Orestes* the writer included a variation on a stroboscope consisting of a disc with holes rotated in front of a spotlight. It should be remembered that members of an audience can take very little of such a flashing light without becoming annoyed and uncomfortable. Another interesting effect was tried in the same production during a choral interlude, where an overhead projector with a double polaroid disc provided an appropriate color-changing pattern on the area where the chorus danced. Between the polaroid discs nothing more than a piece of crumpled cellophane was needed.

A recent production of *Rosencrantz and Guildenstern Are Dead* had an acting area of steps and platforms. The background was a book-shaped projection screen on which all of the scenic forms were projected from a 35-mm projector. This trend in providing projected backgrounds or in superimposing projections on scenic backgrounds is common both here and in Europe. Theatres in Germany and Czechoslovakia have been leaders in this movement. Sometimes many projection screens of different shapes have been a part of the overall design, and both front and rear projections have been combined in new and startling ways. The appearance of the actor may be distorted and his facial expression sacrificed temporarily in order to produce a startling effect. In the contemporary theatre there is an increasing trend toward experimentation in staging practice. Complex patterns of light in space and on backgrounds are increasingly a part of this new direction, often along psychedelic lines.

CONCLUSION

This chapter attempts to show how the instruments (Chapter 4) and control equipment (Chapter 8) can be applied to the practice of lighting a play using the principles of illumination (Chapter 3), electricity (Chapter 7), and color (Chapter 6). Furthermore, the philosophy and analysis of lighting the stage (Chapter 9) have been pulled together in general and then in specific examples of lighting practice both in the academic theatre and the commercial theatre.

Figure 9–13 A scene from Paul Green's *Sing All a Green Willow*. The Carolina Playmakers, University of North Carolina. Design by Tom Rezzuto.

Figure 9–14   A scene from Strindberg's *The Dream Play*. University Theatre, University of Iowa. Design by Thadeus Torp. Lighting by David Thayer.

Through a discussion of several examples on different stages it is hoped that many of the problems confronting the student of stage lighting will have been anticipated. One of the fascinations of this field is that it is almost never routine and that each new production is a challenge with some novel aspect, something aesthetic and stimulating to the imagination. New equipment, new methods, exchanges of ideas with fellow artists—all should lead us further into the art of lighting for the actor, the background, and the play.

GLOSSARY OF STAGE LIGHTING TERMS

(For more elaborate definitions and descriptions of the following terms and others in the text, see the index.)

Acting area   That portion of the stage enclosed by scenery which is used by the actors during a performance.

Alzak   A patented method of processing aluminum reflecting surfaces to increase reflectance and to prevent deterioration. It is now used in many lighting instruments.

Ampere   The common unit of current or rate of flow of electricity.

Arc light   Any lighting instrument, usually a follow spotlight or outdoor parallel beam parabolic reflector (searchlight), employing a carbon arc light source. The power supply may be either direct or alternating current, but direct current is more satisfactory.

Autotransformer   A transformer in which a single coil of wire wound around an iron core is used as both primary and secondary. As used in the theatre for a dimmer, it has a brush that can be rotated around the coil, thus changing the voltage applied to the lamps.

Baby spotlight   A small spotlight intended for a 100-, 250-, or 400-watt lamp. Its lens is ordinarily 5 inches, 4½ inches, or smaller in diameter.

Backing   A drop, a border, or a tab used to limit the audience's view through an opening (e.g., a doorway) in a set of scenery.

Backing striplight   A short, light striplight about 3 feet long or less, wired in one circuit and used to light backings behind doors and so on. It is sometimes used between ground rows.

Balcony spotlight   A spotlight mounted somewhere in the balcony of the auditorium, frequently on a railing or in a box at the front of the balcony.

Base   (1) The part of an incandescent lamp that screws into, or is fastened in, the socket or receptacle. (2) A cast-iron disc that can be attached to the yoke of a spotlight to make the spotlight sit on a flat surface.

Beam   The cone of light from a lens or a parabolic reflector.

Beam light   A spotlight mounted in a false beam or otherwise concealed in the auditorium ceiling for the purpose of lighting the downstage acting areas from above. Anteproscenium light is a synonym.

Blackout   A rapid change in illumination produced by opening a switch, usually a master switch, to control all or nearly all of the illumination on the stage.

197

Board   See *Control board.*

Boomerang   A box attached to a lighting instrument to hold color frames. Its purpose is to make color changes convenient, and frequently the frames can be changed electrically or mechanically at a distance.

Borderlight   A striplight, usually as long as the width of the proscenium arch, hung overhead from the gridiron to produce general illumination on the stage. Many older theatres had three or four of them hung at intervals of 10 to 12 feet.

Bridge   A narrow platform, as long or longer than the width of the proscenium arch, hung from the gridiron or sometimes supported from the side walls or on legs. Various kinds of lighting instruments are mounted on the upstage side of the bridge, and an operator can adjust them or change color frames from the platform just behind the instruments. If a theatre has only one bridge, it is usually hung just upstage from the teaser.

Brightness   That property of any color that allows the color to be classified according to a series of grays ranging from black to white. Lightness is used as a synonym.

Bulb   The glass part of an incandescent lamp containing the filament, supports, and so on.

Cable   An electrical conductor (two or three wires in each cable is the usual practice on the stage) containing one or more copper wires properly insulated with cotton and rubber or plastic and further protected on the outside with a very tough rubber or neoprene sheath to withstand rough treatment.

Circuit   A complete path of good conductors leading from the source of electrical energy to a useful device, such as a lighting instrument, and back again to the source.

Circuit breaker   A more modern device for opening a circuit automatically, taking the place of a fuse.

Clamp, or Pipe clamp   A brass, aluminum, or steel device that connects the yoke or pipe arm of a spotlight or other instrument to a pipe batten.

Code   Refers to the National Electrical Code, or to the city electrical code that has been enacted into law and based on the National Electrical Code.

Color   In general, refers to all sensations arising from activity of the retina. Color may be chromatic or achromatic, the latter including white, grays, and black.

Color frame   A metal, wood, or cardboard holder to keep the color filter rigid and to protect it when placed in a lighting instrument.

Color medium or filter   A transparent material such as glass, gelatin, or sheet plastic used to obtain color from incandescent light by a process called selective transmission.

Complements, or Complementary colors   Two colors possessing hue that may be mixed to produce white light. Transparent complementary pigments mixed together produce gray.

Connector   A small block of insulating material with metallic contacts connected to the ends of cable or to lighting instruments, so that power may be conducted from an outlet on the stage through one or more cables to a lighting instrument. Connectors are of two kinds, the line connector, which is at the "hot" or power end, and the load connector, which is fastened to an instrument or the instrument end of a cable. The Twistlock connector is now common.

Console   The modern term for the manually operated portion of a remote-control lighting system. It is usually placed at the rear of the auditorium, where the operator has full view of the stage. This desk-like arrangement contains the switch and dimmer controls that remotely control the actual dimmers and switches.

Contactor   A magnetically operated switch, located in a remote place to save space and to keep the noise of closing the contractor from being heard on the stage. A small switch on the manually operated pilot control board is used to energize the magnet that closes the contactor.

Control board   The distribution point of electrical energy where the amount of energy going to the various lighting instruments on the stage may be controlled. It is composed of switches and dimmers, as well as necessary wiring for the proper distribution of power.

Cue sheet   A record of the dimmer readings and changes for each scene of the play, placed on the control board or console where the operator can see it during the progress of a performance.

Current   Rate of flow of electricity is called current of electricity. It is expressed in amperes.

Cyclorama   A large curtain of canvas, or other material—single or in sections—hung from a horizonal U-shaped wood or metal frame (pipe) suspended by sets of lines from the gridiron.

Diffuse reflection   Reflection in all directions.

Dim   To change the amount of illumination, either by increasing it or decreasing it.

Dimmer   Any means for changing the amount of light, but usually an electrical device operating on the principle of resistance, reactance, autotransformer, electronic tube, magnetic amplifier, or thyrister.

Effect machine   See *Sciopticon* or *Lens projector*.

Electrician   A name applied in the professional theatre to a union stage-hand who is capable of operating the control board and of making connections between instruments and the electrical outlets. The term is correctly applied to one who is capable of wiring buildings and of making and repairing various kinds of electrical apparatus.

Ellipsoidal reflector   A reflector used in spotlights and floodlights that has two focal points. When a light source is placed at one focal point, light falling on the surface of the reflector converges to the other focal point.

Fireplace effects   A papier-mâché, wood, or metal combination of logs or coal grate home-made or purchased from a manufacturer of fireplace accessories. These devices contain small incandescent lamps and simulate a fireplace fire in an interior setting; sometimes they are made in the form of a "campfire" for exteriors.

Floodlight A lighting instrument composed chiefly of a large reflector and a fairly high-wattage lamp. It is used to produce general illumination.

Floor pocket A metal box in the stage floor, its top flush with the floor surface, in which the stage electrical outlets are placed.

Fluorescence Some substances have the property of absorbing invisible light and emitting visible light. This property is called fluorescence. Because the emitted light is very dim it can be noticed only in dark surroundings.

Focus The point to which parallel rays of light converge after passing through a lens. As a verb it is frequently used on the stage to refer to the adjustment of a spotlight to make the illuminated area larger or smaller.

Foot-candle A unit of illumination. The illumination on a surface when there is a luminous flux of 1 lumen on an area of 1 square foot. It is also the illumination on a surface 1 foot from a source of 1 candela.

Footlights One or more striplights placed in a recess or trough outside the curtain line to produce general illumination from below.

Fresnel The name applied to a common type of lens that employs the outer ring portion of several plano-convex lenses cast into one flat unit of glass with a small plano-convex lens at the center. All of the elements usually have approximately the same focal length. The name comes from a French scientist.

Funnel A sheet-metal hood, circular or square in section, from 1 to 3 feet long, intended to absorb spill or stray light that would otherwise fall outside the illuminated area. The funnel is fastened to the front of a spotlight (usually called high hat).

Fuse A protective device used in main circuits and branch circuits to prevent overloads and short circuits that might damage electrical equipment. When an overload occurs, the small strip of fusable metal (within the fuse) melts and breaks the circuits.

Gelatin The most common color medium. It is made of ordinary gelatin in thin sheets with an aniline dye producing the color.

Glare The cause of the sensation of discomfort experienced when observing a surface or light source that is very bright. It depends on contrasts as well as the intrinsic brightness of a source or surface.

Grand master A term applied to a switch or dimmer that controls all of the individual switches or dimmers. It is used in contrast to a group master which may master a smaller number of individual controls. System master is a synonym.

Group master A master dimmer that controls fewer dimmers than the whole control board. Group masters ordinarily control from four to 12 individual dimmers.

House lights Auditorium lighting.

Hue   That property of any color that distinguishes it from gray of the same brilliance.

Illumination   Strictly, it is the density of the luminous flux on a surface and is expressed in foot-candles. In a general way it is often used as a synonym for lighting.

Illumination meter   A meter that measures illumination, usually read in foot-candles.

Instrument, or Lighting instrument   A synonym for lighting unit, as a spotlight, striplight, floodlight, and so on.

Insulation   Materials, such as fabric, rubber, fiber, porcelain, and so forth that are very poor conductors of electricity and are used to prevent conductors of opposite polarity from coming in contact with each other, and to prevent contact with individuals who must handle the conductors.

Intensity   The power of a light source, measured in candelas.

Interlock   To move several dimmer handles up or down together mechanically. The usual method is to have a catch that temporarily connects each handle to a single shaft. A single handle permanently fastened to the shaft will then control any of the individural handles connected to it.

Lamp, or Incandescent lamp   Refers to the complete unit, including bulb, base, filament, lead-in wires, and so forth.

Lamp dip, or Colored lacquer   A colored transparent or frosted lacquer used on clear or frosted incandescent lamps when it is difficult to place color media in front of them.

Left stage   Any position on the stage to one's left when facing the audience.

Lens   A piece of transparent material, such as glass, frequently having one or two spherical surfaces and sometimes having cylindrical surfaces. Lenses are used on the stage to converge the rays of light from a small source and concentrate the light to a narrow beam. They are used also to produce an image from a lantern slide or of moving objects. The latter are called objective or projection lenses; the former, condensing lenses.

Lens projector   A scenic slide projector provided with a large-wattage lamp (1000 to 5000 watts), condensing lenses, blowers, and a short focal length objective lens to project scenic elements to a drop or cyclorama. Some have a motor-driven accessory to move a film strip vertically or horizontally, for example, the projection of moving clouds.

Lighting unit   See *Instrument.*

Linnebach projector, or Shadowgraph projector   A sheet-metal hood painted black inside, using a concentrated source of light and a transparent painted or cut-out slide.

Louvers, or Spill shields   A series of thin cylindrical sections of sheet metal or parallel strips, placed in front of a reflector to eliminate spill light or direct emanation that would fall outside the beam produced by the reflector.

Lumen   The unit of luminous flux. The flux through a unit solid angle (steradian) from a source of 1 candela. It is also the flux on a surface 1 square foot in area, 1 foot from a source of 1 candela.

Mask   To conceal a lighting instrument from the audience, usually by means of scenery.

Master dimmer, or Switch   See *Grand master.*

Multiple, or Parallel circuit   A circuit in which there are several paths through which the current may flow, as in all stage lighting circuits and, in fact, nearly all lighting circuits except street lighting.

Objective lens   See *Lens.*

Olivette   A box floodlight that can be mounted on a stand or hung by means of chains from a pipe batten.

Operating light   Usually a work light built into the control board to illuminate the handles and the cue sheet.

Operator   Any person who handles lighting instruments and equipment on the stage, or changes color frames between scenes. A person in charge of the control board for a production is frequently called the control board operator.

Outlet   A receptacle into which a plug or connector is inserted in order to connect a lighting instrument to the source of electrical energy. A floor pocket or wall pocket may contain one or more outlets.

Parabolic reflector   A concave reflector whose surface is in the form of a paraboloid. When a source of light is placed at the focus, reflected rays of light tend to go out in straight lines. It is used in floodlights and striplights.

Parallel circuit   See *Multiple circuit.*

Phosphorescence   A substance is said to exhibit the property of phosphorescence if, after exposure to light, it continues to give off visible light when the stimulating source has been removed.

Pilot light   A small incandescent lamp, frequently covered with a colored cap, placed in the face of a control board to indicate that a circuit is turned on. One is frequently placed beside the switch and dimmer handle of each individual circuit.

Pipe batten   A length of pipe suspended on a set of lines. Flied scenery is frequently attached to a pipe batten by means of snatch lines instead of being tied directly to a set of lines. A pipe batten is a standard part in a unit of the counterweight system. It is also used to carry lighting instruments.

Pipe clamp   See *Clamp.*

Plug   A standard stage plug is a fiber block with heavy copper contacts rated for 50 amperes. It fits into a standard stage outlet. Especially in the nonprofessional theatre, these plugs and outlets are being replaced by 15- or 30-ampere stage connectors or Twistlock connectors.

Pocket   See *Floor pocket.*

Portable control board   A control board intended to be moved about, especially from one theatre to another.

Primary colors   The primary colors in light (additive) are usually called blue, green, and red. The primary colors in pigments (subtractive) are commonly considered to be blue-green, yellow, and magenta.

Projector   A floodlight with a polished parabolic reflector and concentric louvers producing a beam of light is often called a floodlight projector or parallel beam projector. See also *Lens* and *Linnebach projector.*

Quality   In light it is sometimes used as a synonym for color.

Receptacle   See *Outlet.* Frequently used as a synonym for socket.

Reflectance   The reflected light divided by the incident light, usually expressed in percent.

Reflector   Any surface that reflects light, but this term usually refers to a definite piece of equipment, such as a spotlight reflector.

Regular reflection   Reflection in which the angle of incidence is equal to the angle of reflection. Examples are highly polished metals and glass mirrors.

Remote control   Control in which the current through the lamps does not pass through the manually operated control board, but through dimmers and switches in some remote place such as the basement of the theatre. Its purpose is to make possible the use of small and compact parts in the manually operated pilot control board (console).

Resistance   A characteristic of materials concerned with their ability to conduct electricity. Insulating materials are said to have very high resistance and conductors very low resistance.

Rheostat   A variable resistance. Sometimes a synonym for resistance dimmer.

Saturation   That property of any color possessing hue which determines its degree of difference from gray of the same brightness. A measure of amount of hue.

Sciopticon   A spotlight to which has been added a supplementary condensing lens, moving-effect holder, and an objective lens. Such moving effects as clouds, rain, rippling water, and so on are accomplished with this instrument.

Series circuit   A circuit with a single path in which the same current passes through every element.

Shade   In reference to color, a shade is a color below median gray in lightness and frequently, but not necessarily, low in saturation.

Short circuit   When two wires of opposite polarity and low resistance come in contact, the current tends to become excessive and dangerous, possibly causing fire or damage to electrical equipment and wiring. Fuses or circuit breakers are used to prevent damage when this accidental condition obtains.

Spherical reflector   A concave reflector that has the property of sending back light to the center of curvature when a source of light is placed at this center. It is used in spotlights and, combined with a parabolic shape, in striplights.

Spill, or Spill light   Stray light outside a beam, or any light that is misplaced on scenery or other objects on the stage.

Spotlight   A lighting instrument with a condensing lens producing a beam of light; used for specific illumination.

Stand   A heavy round iron base to which is attached vertical telescoping pipes. Spotlights and floodlights can be attached to the end of the inner pipe and directed toward the acting area from a position 5 or 10 feet above the floor. Some have triangular bases and casters.

Striplight   A short row of spherical parabolic reflectors or R40 lamps, usually 6 feet long but obtainable in any length. They are usually wired in three circuits and have connectors at both ends to be connected end to end, primarily to light the cyclorama from the stage floor. These can be arranged as borderlights to light drops and also as footlights when needed.

Switch   A device used to open and close an electrical circuit. In modern stage lighting practice, switches are placed behind the face of a control board with the handle extending through to the front. A remote-control switch is called a contactor or magnetic switch.

Switchboard   See *Control board*. The term switchboard came into use when dimmers were considered less important than switches. Switchboard as a term for control board is going out of use.

Throw   Indicates the distance from a lighting instrument to the illuminated area.

Tint   A color higher in brightness than median gray and of various degrees of saturation.

Tormentor light   A spotlight mounted on a verticle pipe batten just off-stage from either tormentor.

Work light   Illumination for the stage used for rehearsals, scene shifting, and building. Work light is controlled ordinarily by a wall switch on the stage.

X-Ray   Once the trade name for a particular type of borderlight, it is still used occasionally to refer to the first borderlight or striplights on the first pipe.

SELECTED BIBLIOGRAPHY

Appia, A., *A Work of Living Art and Man is the Measure of All Things* (Coral Gables, Fla.: University of Miami Press, 1960).

Appia, A., *Music and the Art of the Theatre*, edited by Barnard Hewett (Coral Gables, Fla.: University of Miami Press, 1962).

Bellman, W. F., *Lighting the Stage* (San Francisco: Chandler, 1967).

Bentham, Frederick, *Stage Lighting* (London: Pitman, 1950). A British text, particulary good on equipment.

Bentham, Frederick, *The Art of Stage Lighting* (London: Pitman, 1968).

Billmeyer, Fred W., Jr., and Saltzman, Max, *Principles of Color Technology* (New York: Wiley, 1966).

Bowman, Wayne, *Modern Theatre Lighting* (New York: Harper, 1957).

Clark, C. N., *Characteristics of Incandescent Lamps for Theatre Stages, Television and Film Studios* (Reprinted from *Illuminating Engineering*, LXI, 7, July 1966).

Color As Light (New York: International Printing Ink Corp., 1935). An elementary monograph on the physics of color.

Corry, P., *Lighting the Stage*, 3rd ed. (London: Pitman, 1962).

Engel, Alfred von, *Bühnenbeleuchtung* (Leipzig: Hachmeister, 1926). Profusely illustrated.

Evans, Ralph M., *An Introduction to Color* (New York: Wiley, 1948). A thorough, well-written discussion of the physics and psychophysics of color.

Fuchs, Theodore, *Home-Built Lighting Equipment* (New York: French, 1939).

Fuchs, Theodore, *Stage Lighting* (New York: Blom, 1964). Reprint. A comprehensive treatment of the subject with special emphasis on equipment; now primarily of historical interest.

Gassner, John, *Producing the Play*, rev. ed. (New York: Holt, 1953). Several chapters on stage lighting.

Godlove, I. H., *Bibliography on Color: Inter-Society Color Council* (c/o Braden Sutphin Ink Co., Cleveland, Ohio, 1957).

Hartman, Louis, *Theatre Lighting: A Manual of the Stage Switchboard* (New York: Appleton-Century, 1930). Interesting reminiscences of the manner in which Belasco and Hartman achieved their effects.

Heffner, Hubert C., Selden, Samuel, and Sellman, Hunton D., *Modern Theatre Practice*, 4th ed. (New York: Appleton-Century-Crofts, 1959). The lighting portion is a little more elementary than *Essentials of Stage Lighting*.

Hewitt, Barnard, Foster, J. F., and Wolle, Muriel S., *Play Production: Theory and Practice* (Philadelphia: Lippincott, 1952).

Jacobson, Egbert, *Basic Color: An Interpretation of the Ostwald Color System* (Chicago: Theobald, 1948).

Knapp, Jack Stuart, *Lighting the Stage with Homemade Equipment* (Boston: Baker, 1933).

Kranich, Frederick, *Bühnentechnik der Gegenwart* (Berlin: 1929 and 1933). Profusely illustrated. One can learn much about German and theatre practice from the illustrations in this and the Engel volume, even if he cannot read German. This volume covers every aspect of theatre engineering, including large sections on lighting.

Light Sources Past and Present, LS 139 (General Electric Co., 1956). Useful for those interested in lamp history and recent design.

Light Measurement and Control, G.E. Bulletin, TP-118 (General Electric Co., March 1965).

Light and Color, G.E. Bulletin, TP-119 (General Electric Co., August 1967).

Luckiesh, Matthew, *Light and Shade and Their Application* (New York: Van Nostrand, 1917). Good general background material.

Luckiesh, Matthew, *Color and Its Application*, 2nd ed. (New York: Van Nostrand, 1921).

McCandless, Stanley R., *Method of Lighting the Stage*, 4th ed. (New York, Theatre Arts, 1958).

McCandless, Stanley R., *A Syllabus of Stage Lighting*, 9th ed. (New Haven, Conn.: Yale University Press, 1958). A sound, thorough text.

Moyer, Jason A., and Wostrel, John F., *Industrial Electricity and Wiring* (New York: McGraw-Hill, 1943).

Munsell, A. H., *A Color Notation* (Munsell Color Co., Baltimore, Md., 1936–1963).

Optical Society of America, Committee on Colorimetry, *The Science of Color* (New York: Crowell, 1953–1963).

Parker, W. O., and Smith, H. K., *Scene Design and Stage Lighting*, 2nd ed. (New York: Holt, 1968).

Ridge, C. Harold, and Aldred, F. S., *Stage Lighting Principles and Practice* (London: Pitman, 1940). A good British text, interesting largely for British terminology.

Rubin, Joel E., and Watson, Leland H., *Theatrical Lighting Practice* (New York: Theatre Arts, 1954). Covers arena, outdoor production, and television as well as stage lighting.

Staley, Karl A., *Fundamentals of Light and Lighting*, G. E. Bulletin LD2 (General Electric Co., 1960). Contains a useful discussion of the physics of light.

Weitz, C. E., *Lamp Bulletin*, G.E. Bulletin LD1 (General Electric Co., 1956). Characteristics and applications of various incandescent lamps and other light sources.

Wilfred, Thomas, *Projected Scenery, A Technical Manual* (West Nyack, N.Y.: Art Institute of Light, 1955).

Williams, R. Gillespie, *The Technique of Stage Lighting* (London: Pitman, 1952). A British text, good on color and British practice.

Williams, R. Gillespie, *Lighting for Color and Form: Principles, Equipment and Applications* (London: Pitman, 1954).

DIRECTORY OF
MANUFACTURERS

Berkey-Color Tran., Inc., 1015 Chestnut St., Burbank, Calif. Photographic and television lighting equipment.

Brigham Gelatin Co., Randolph, Vt. Colored, clear, and frosted sheet gelatin.

Buhl Optical Co., 1009 Beech Ave., Pittsburg, Pa.

Century Strand, Inc., 3411 W. El Segundo Blvd., Hawthorne, Calif.

Electro Controls, Inc., 2975 S. Second West St., Salt Lake City, Utah.

General Electric Company, Large Lamp Department, Nela Park, Cleveland, Ohio. Lamps.

General Radio Co., 300 Baker Ave., Concord, Mass. *Variac* autotransformer dimmers.

Hub Electric Co., Inc., 940 Industrial Drive, Elmhurst, Ill. Control boards and general lighting equipment.

Kliegl Bros., 32-32 48th Ave., Long Island City, N.Y. General lighting equipment and control boards.

Kliegl Bros. Western Corp., 2333 N. Valley Ct., Burbank, Calif.

Major Corporation, 4620 W. Fullerton Ave., Chicago, Ill. Instruments and control equipment.

Mole-Richardson Co., 937 N. Sycamore Ave., Hollywood, Calif. Motion picture lighting equipment.

Paramount Cosmetics and Theatrical Make-up, 3710 Hudson Ave., Union City, N.J.

Rosco Laboratories Inc., 36 Bush Ave., Port Chester, N.Y. Colored gelatin and plastic sheets.

Shannon Luminous Materials Co., 7356 Santa Monica Blvd., Hollywood, Calif.

Skirpan Lighting Control Corp., 41-43 24th St., Long Island City, N.Y. Lighting control equipment.

Strand Electric and Engineering Co., Ltd., 3201 N. Highway 100, Minneapolis, Minn.; 105 Davenport Rd., Toronto, Ont.; 29 King St., London, W.C. 2, England. England's largest lighting equipment manufacturer.

Stroblite Co., Inc., 29 W. 15th St., New York, N.Y. Ultraviolet effects and materials.

Strong Electric Corp., 176 City Park Ave., Toledo, Ohio. Arc and incandescent follow spotlights and slide projectors.

Superior Electric Co., 97 Lee Ave., Bristol, Conn. Powerstat dimmers and packaged control boards.

Sylvania Electric Products Inc., Lighting Products Division, 60 Boston St., Salem Mass. Lamps.

Sylvania Lighting Products, Group, 100 Endicott St., Danvers, Mass.

Theatre Production Service, 59 Fourth Ave., New York, N.Y.

Trans-Lux News Sign Corp., 625 Madison Avenue, New York, N.Y. Projectors and projection screens.

Ward Leonard Electric Company, 45 South Street, Mount Vernon, N.Y. Autotransformer and SCR dimmers and other control devices.

Westinghouse Electric Corp., Lamp Parts Dept., Bloomfield, N.J. Lamps.

INDEX